NETWORK MARKETING
$ECRET$
—— FROM ——
TOP EARNERS

YOUR SUCCESS BLUEPRINT

TGON Publishing

TGON Publishing

Print ISBN: 978-1-7358447-1-8
eBook ISBN: 978-1-7358447-2-5

CONTENTS

INTRODUCTION

I am going to let you in on a little secret ...

Sure, I am the coach who gets the opportunity to personally work with many of the very top earners in the network marketing industry ... but I am the one who learns the most. Top leaders come to me for personal coaching, consulting, and masterminds. I coach many of these leaders one on one, and I have them at my six- and seven-figure masterminds. I am always blown away by what I learn from them, both personally and professionally. Each time I work with a top leader, I gain more information from them on what is working out in the field. That is why this industry works so well; because leaders are willing to share. They are willing to go out and try new things then come back and report. The best leaders that I have worked with are the ones that share openly and authentically.

As I went through several edits of this book, I was again impressed with the incredible value each one of these leaders provided. These leaders are all co-authors of this book. They are not your average leaders. They have all had massive success. They are from all over the world with completely different backgrounds, ages, and races.

Collectively, we are giving you some of the best strategies in all of network marketing. DO NOT JUST READ THIS BOOK! Study it. Take notes throughout and create what I call your executables. Executables are *your* action steps. What are you going to implement from this book? That's the question you should be asking yourself throughout the book. Ideas are great, but the execution of those ideas is everything. At the end of every single chapter, you should have one to two executables that you can start today. USE the strategies, tips, and tools in this book to help you create a successful network marketing business. Use the book so that YOU can be one of the next leaders in an upcoming book.

The ability to learn how to learn is the greatest ability one can have. I challenge you to write down the key things you will execute from this book. Once you finish this book, go to your notes and prioritize them in order. If you do, this book could become that life-changing book that helps you have that BREAKTHROUGH!

Rob Sperry

Author: Shayo Alofe

- Earned my first six figures, with my first company, just nine months after joining the business.

- Highest ranked in the UK in three companies so far.

- Built a team of 20,000+ distributors and customers, across six countries, in two years and seven months.

"If you can see it in your mind, you can hold it in your hands."

I felt the desire to be a successful businesswoman even as a young girl growing up in Nigeria. My parents are both academics, so I was raised in a household where education was important. They were both lecturers, and it was known that getting a masters was expected in our family. I didn`t go down that road because that desire to make my own path and pursue business continued to grow throughout my life.

After we relocated to the UK in 2002, it was a complete accident that in 2006 I found network marketing. I was sitting at my desk job, as a project management professional, wondering how I could have more time with my family. I was making great money as a project management professional, but the time freedom wasn`t there. I had kids and I was missing their childhood as I sat at that desk. It just didn`t feel right. I wanted to be the one to drop my kids off at school and pick them up. I wanted to be the one they were excited to talk to, not the nanny.

I searched "work from home" on Google, and I was shocked at what popped up! There are people right now that are also wondering how to have more time freedom. I was intrigued by what I found. When I read about network marketing, it made sense to me and really spoke to who I am.

I love to refer people to products, services, or experiences I love. If I buy something that works, I will tell everyone. If I watch a movie I enjoy, I want to spread the news. That is just the type of person I am. When I saw that this is what network marketing really is– you find a product you love, tell people about it, and get paid–I thought, "WOW, this is me." I would tell anybody who would listen to everything that worked for me. To get paid for it just made sense. Network marketing was perfect for my personality.

There are people right now, searching on the internet, trying to figure out how to spend more time with their kids or make more money. How are you going to be the solution for someone searching for answers? That is a question you need to ask yourself as you get started in network marketing.

I thought at the time that my big reason for doing this business was time freedom with my kids. As I look back, I see that I needed network marketing to help me get out of a far worse situation that my past self couldn't get out of on her own. I was married for thirteen years, and nine of those years involved physical abuse.

During some of those years I was doing network marketing and building businesses. When I filed for divorce, and my decree of absolute came, I looked at that journey and wondered how I survived the abuse at the hands of someone who was supposed to love me the most. I was building a six-figure-a-year business as well as building teams. The personal growth I went through helped me survive and thrive enough to leave. My teams never knew what I was going through. I became strong, resilient, and I could face anything that was coming. I learned to grow by dealing with the things I was going through. I am so thankful for this industry. This industry helped me stand up to my abuser.

There are people struggling right now and not knowing how they are going to face their problems. Network marketing has got you! Read this chapter. Read this book. Believe in yourself enough to take these tips and strategies; use them to grow a business that not only helps you create time freedom, but soul freedom.

Coaches Notes: I have been able to hear Shayo speak a few different times in Europe. Shayo uses her personal struggles as the reason for her success, not as the excuse for potential failures. If you were to sit down with each person you know, you would find that all of us have struggles. The difference between those who are successful and those who aren`t is the story they tell themselves. If you use your struggles as learning opportunities, you just keep getting better. Here is some tough love. You can make excuses or you can make money, but you can`t make both. Be like Shayo and use those trials to strengthen you.

Your Very First Step

When I started with my first network marketing company, I just wanted the product. I wasn't interested in joining the company. The woman I contacted was going to be driving quite some distance to drop my order off; I didn't want her to waste her time driving, and I didn't want to miss an opportunity to share a product I loved with my friends. I told her to bring some extra product and I would invite some of my friends over.

I texted fifty women, and told them that this woman was coming over. Ten ladies showed up that snowy, Saturday morning in February. These ladies were beyond excited. They were acting like teenagers! At the end of the day, six out of the ten women wanted to do the business. The lady, I had contacted, asked me again if I wanted to do the business. At that point, I said, "OK, six people want to do this. I am in."

It's easy for me to invite fifty people to an event. That is my nature. I am a talker. I can talk to anyone about anything! Not everyone has that. I couldn't base my success solely on my personality. I realized that my network is large because I am a big personality that draws people in.

Building a network doesn't only come from personality. You can use the network you have now and build a bigger network with your own personality. It is a simple thing that everyone can do and still get results, regardless of your personality or experience. It shouldn't make a difference at all. Be willing to take an interest in others.

When I texted fifty women to come to my house and check out the product, I wasn`t interested in me. I was interested in them. I wanted to share something that I thought they would love. It was about them. Create genuine interest in others.

If you don`t have people, go and find them. You have to increase people in your phone contacts and on social media. Start to make the connections authentically. Talk about your life, your culture, your kids, whatever–just connect with people. You will get to a point that people are comfortable enough to reach out and see what you are doing. It is that simple.

It is about increasing your contacts first. Some say that they don`t have 200 people on their phone. That isn`t going to work. What we do is a numbers game. I tell people to get 100 people on their phone contact list, and then we can start the business. It is the very first step. Be committed enough to create a contact list of one hundred people. If you only have twenty people to reach out to, and you aren`t willing to get to know more people, you aren`t going to have success.

Coaches Notes: Your customers are your biggest goldmine! So many network marketers tell me they want more business builders, but they don`t realize that their current customers are their best business builders. I`m not saying you should try to force every single customer to become a business builder, by any means. I`m saying when people genuinely like your products, they will naturally share with others. They are doing the business without even knowing it. Think about it. When you love a good movie, you tell others about it without any prompting whatsoever. It is a natural process. By making your customers more of a focus, you will be able to tap into their networks. Many, like Shayo, will see the business opportunity and jump in as a distributor. Learn more about this at www.sperrybonus.com

Simple Steps Duplicate

When you start out, keep it simple so that everyone around you sees how easy it is. When I showed people what I was doing, I would have them say, "If Shayo can do that, I can too!" That is the goal. Make it so simple that people can see themselves doing it.

When I learned about duplication and keeping it simple, my business skyrocketed. I had joined another company and was looking for simple steps that duplicated. My mentor and I asked the question, "How can we create a simple system, to build this business, that people can follow step by step and know what results they could be getting?"

I started to get things together in a simple system and we rolled it out. I was amazed by the results. Even my mentor was shocked. I was just an excitable, young girl who was trying to find her own foot in the business. After four months, our team had grown to over 4,000 people in sixteen countries. That was it for me. I finally understood why we need duplication in network marketing, and how it wasn`t based on me.

Eric Worre said, "If it doesn`t duplicate, don`t do it." It`s not about what works, it`s about what duplicates. Some people have different ideas, like putting an advert on the radio. That will never duplicate. Have a simple system like a text message you can send to people, and show them a tool which presents the overview to those people. Take yourself out of the equation.

Consistency is key. With duplication, you must have a system. Nothing should derail that system. The system has to work, and you must stick to it. You guard that system with your life. If anyone tries to do anything to that system, you stop them immediately and get back to the original system. Be consistent with the system. Make sure the messaging around the system stays positive and that it continues to work. Coach on the system. Everyone can do the system. It is the priority. It takes the person out of the spotlight and puts it on the system.

Sharing Stories System

We have several different systems that we use. You, your mentor, or company are going to have your own system that you can either duplicate or come up with. Don`t overthink it. Do the simple system. Do what your leaders teach you. All of the top leaders have systems. Know the system for your company and do that system. It will work. Systems can be duplicated–humans cannot.

I wanted to share with you one system that has made a huge impact on our team. This is a system that anyone can do. It duplicates to any person and any personality.

The system starts from the very first contact with a prospect. We do it through stories. Share your stories. Share about the single mom that can take her kids on holiday or out to eat. Share about the medical doctor that has been able to start his own practice because of his income from network marketing. When you do that, people recognize themselves in the story. When people have questions, we invite them to a presentation and show them value. Show them the value before the price. If they understand the value, then the price makes sense. If you show them the price first, they don`t listen. They judge it based on the price.

Do the presentation and then do third party validation. Whether that is on a phone call or a WhatsApp group, this is a private space for the prospect to ask questions. We guide them through the next steps and ask them questions. Do they want to be a customer or business partner?

From there, we take them through the system of either customer or business partner. If they are a customer, they order their products and they are put into a customer group on Facebook. There they can access more information and testimonials.

If they become a business partner, they are put into the team Facebook group, their own working group on WhatsApp, and we start their training. It states the whole process including what to do and how to do it. We make it so simple. They don`t have to figure anything out. It is just a copy and paste system. They are copying the system. This works! I have been doing it since I came up with the system.It`s simple. This system works.

Don't Be The Superstar— Create A Galaxy

With a traditional business, you can be the star. You can be the one who is great at sales and marketing, and that`s fine. You can`t do that in network marketing. The bigger and better your network is, the better *everyone* does. It is not about being the lone star or superstar; it is about creating a galaxy of stars. If you do it all yourself, there is no leverage. You need leverage. You need different skills from different people.

Being the super star, people shout your name and they may look up to you, but you aren`t going to be loved and admired by them. Because you haven`t helped them make their dreams come true. They think you are the only one that can do it. They think you have a special touch. That isn`t how network marketing works. It is about helping everybody become somebody. It is about the system that can be duplicated, and it can help you do that.

It is about supporting and raising leaders from the start, by using the system. When you have that in place, you can put them in the system and let it work to mentor leaders. You can identify the up and coming people ,so much faster, in a system and start reaching out to help them. You then teach them how to do it.

Putting the spotlight on others will create a great culture. It isn`t just about you. You are one of the bright and shining stars in the galaxy. Be a dream builder. Help people build their dreams by building them up first. Then they start to attract the right people to help support and build their dreams. It helps to surround yourself with great people. It starts by not making it all about you.

I see my entire team as a blessing. They could be at any company, on any team; it is a privilege and honor to have them on our team and be able to be around them. I am invested in their dreams.

Find your own path to success, but use a system that duplicates to create success. People try to make it so complicated. This business is simple. When we keep it that way, more people are open and willing to try. Don`t block the blessings by making it hard.

My daughter said the other day, "I am so proud of you." That is a huge deal coming from a teenager! I have become the type of woman that my daughter is proud of. That is the gift of network marketing and the business. Use the simple systems to become the person that your family is proud of. Become the person that you are proud of. You can do it.

Coaches Notes: You always hear me talk about energy and how the top leaders possess it. Shayo is no different. She has as much contagious energy as anyone you will ever meet. She understands that this business is about empowering others to become better. Good leaders have vision, but great leaders *give* vision. Shayo focuses on making others the superstar. She casts the vision of what they can do. She gives them that belief and confidence. You may not feel adequate to do that yet. If that`s the case, my challenge for you is to always strive to see what people can become rather than seeing them for who they are now. This will help give you that contagious energy and attract better leaders to your business.

Author: Byron Belka

- Network marketing for eighteen years

- Built teams in over fifty different countries worldwide

- CEO and founder of network marketing company

- Been able to live and travel around the world with his wife and kids

"Successful people compress more activity into tighter time frames during critical junctures in their business career."

-My mentor

Action And Story

I love success stories, and people are so motivational to me. As much as I love the success stories, I sometimes find myself being frustrated after reading about people and their success. They have told me all about what they did, but they don`t tell me HOW they did it. I have always been the person that wants the process. I would never leave my readers without the how, because really, that`s the best part!

I`m going to tell you a little bit about myself, and I am going to tell you how I have been able to see success in network marketing. Stories are important, but systems are what you can walk away with and start using in your own business immediately.

I`ve been in this amazing industry for eighteen years. I started when I was twenty-six years old and hit the top level of my first company, when I was twenty-eight. I`m an international business builder who has opened, traveled to, and built teams in over fifty different countries. I`ve even moved and lived overseas with my family, to expand my business. I`ve built teams of hundreds of thousands of people that have done hundreds of millions of dollars in sales. Not only am I a multiple seven figure earner as a distributor, but I am also an owner and founder of a successful networking company. I tell you that really quick because I want you to know that the principles that I`m going to be talking about are what I had to learn through experience.

In this chapter, I`m going to teach you a powerful equation. Something so powerful that when you understand and implement the equation, it will be life changing for your business. It will make sure that your energy and effort is magnified and multiplied. It`ll make sure that you create a stable organization, and it will also ensure that you have unlimited leads.

Coaches Notes: Ten years ago, I went to lunch with Byron Belka. I had heard all about his incredible success. I had heard that he knew how to really sponsor someone`s circle of influence. So much so, that he had built teams all over the world. I still remember that lunch. I was so excited to pick his brain about his strategies. Distributors sign up other distributors ... Leaders launch teams. Leaders discover the strategies to sponsor an individual`s circle of influence. I am grateful that my good friend Byron is able to share his knowledge with you on exactly how these strategies work.

The One Equation You Need In Network Marketing

Like a lot of people, when I started in this industry I didn't realize that it was a different animal. This is a different beast from the regular business model. It has to be learned and when most people join, they start unequipped. They don't have the knowledge, the tools, or the experience to be as effective as they could be. That was me when I joined. I did have a background in sales, so I approached it like a salesperson would. When somebody joined, I checked it off as a sale and I would move on to the next person. I had to learn that in this industry, when you have a new customer or distributor join your team, that's not the end. It's just the beginning.

I sponsored quite a few people and was able to see success, I did some things right based on my understanding as I still hit the top commission level of my company in under two years. That had a lot more to do with me just hustling and working hard than it did about understanding how to build properly. I could have been so much more effective. For the first two years I was doing it wrong. I was trying to find my leaders in the people I personally sponsored rather than understanding there was a faster and better way. There was opportunity right in front of my face that I missed out on because of my lack of understanding, I didn't know it was there. Knowing what I know now I could have helped so many more people and their families.

I was expecting my team to just sponsor people like I was doing. Those that did were the ones I would work with. Those that didn't would most likely quit eventually, as I really didn't understand how I could help them. By not understanding things, I was not helping as many people succeed like I could have, and I was also wasting my time. When you put time and energy into someone, they don`t see results, and they quit without sponsoring others and growing the business: that time and energy is not being magnified. It`s not multiplied and can be considered waste. My hope is for you to learn from this chapter so you can understand these things faster than I did.

At some point, I got smart about what I was creating for myself. When I started to understand the equation that I`m going to share with you, everything changed for me! To create residual income, you need to multiply the energy and effort you put in. You are going to have to put in the time you need to compound and have exponential benefits. If you want the energy and effort you put in to five times itself, 10 times itself, 1000 times itself, it`s only going to happen if you implement this equation into your business practice.

So, what is the equation? It`s CI+DL+LL = SO.

Circle of Influence+Driving Lines+Locking Legs = Strong Solid Successful Organization

I had a multimillionaire mentor who taught me a lot of amazing lessons. One of the things that he taught me changed the game for me. I call it the parachute principle.

The parachute principle comes from a statement that my mentor used to always teach. He would say, "You can parachute me into any country in the world. Give me two weeks, I`ll sponsor a few people and never sponsor again because I`ll drive that team to the center of the earth."

I realized then that I had been bringing people into the business and expecting them to push things forward on their own. I wanted them to figure it out and just follow the systems. I wasn`t creating authentic relationships and mentorships.

The very first step that you need to take right now is to change the way you see people. One person is not just one person in your business, you have one person PLUS their circle of influence. This is the "CI" in the equation. Start shifting to see every single person not as one person in your team, but as a circle of influence, or "CI".

> **Coaches Notes:** Every dud knows a stud. This isn't to judge someone as a human being, but more of a judgment of their skills in this business. This section, which Byron is covering, will truly teach you how to never run out of contacts. Let's break it down a little bit. If someone knows you, then they know others like you. It isn't about just them and their skills, it is about who they know and who those people know. Some studies say that if you know seven people, you know the entire world. Understanding all of this should remind you that recruiting is the most important skill. Recruiting within one's circle of influence is even more effective; these leads are warm leads because they have connections to the person introducing them. Master this skill and you will build a massive team.

It's not one individual in your team that you work with; you actually have one person and everyone they know. When you start to see people as a circle of influence you will be able to help them, and you're better able to focus on the next part of the equation. This is necessary for you to create multiplication of the time and energy that you put into the business.

Think about it. If you evaluate the leaders that you have in your company, or in your own organization, where did they come from? Most of the leaders are not the people that you originally brought into the business. They show up three, four, or five plus levels deep.

Duplication and depth are where the magic happens. If there`s no depth, it`s very difficult to have big things happen in your organization. I have had people, throughout the years, come to me and say, "Byron, I`ve been doing this business for a while, I brought all these people in, and I`m just not getting the results. I`m not making the money that I want."

If I go and look at the structure of their team with them, I already know what I`m going to see. I`m going to see a very shallow organization. What I mean by shallow is there`s no depth. They`ve sponsored people, but the duplication is not happening. If the duplication is not happening, the likelihood of finding that explosive leader in their team is greatly diminished. You must sponsor and HELP that person sponsor. This book is all about recruiting. You are going to learn some amazing stuff, but you must remember that it isn`t about just becoming an amazing recruiter and sponsoring everyone. You must start helping grow other people`s skills and capacities as well.

Direct Sales happen when you sell directly to someone. Networking is when you get people who get people. So you need to be clear and understand exactly what you`re trying to accomplish. You can`t do one thing and expect a different result. You can`t be frustrated that there is no duplication if all you are doing is selling directly to people, without focusing on networking. Look at your business and be honest with yourself. What is it that you are really doing? If you want duplication to happen as a leader, you need to focus on the first part of the equation and help them tap into their circle of influence.

Another way to look at it is when someone joins your team, you need to treat them like a bomb. As soon as they join, the fuse is lit. You now have two weeks before that bomb goes off. To keep them engaged, with their energy and excitement up, they need to have a positive experience and see some type of success during that time frame. If not, you are going to have to spend more time trying to get them excited again.

What do you think is easier? Is it easier to find and sponsor ten individual people to personally enroll?; or is it easier to enroll someone and help them get ten people in their team to sponsor? Which is more stable?

I want you to imagine that you have a goldmine in front of you. There's so much gold in this mine that there's no way that you could mine it all. In fact, you don't even have enough room for all the gold. Now, if this is the case, does it make sense to go out and search for another mine? Why would you go out and look for more gold when you can't even mine what's in front of you?

The problem that most people have is they don't see gold because they are looking at the person as one individual, instead of a circle of influence. They don't know where to look for gold. Even though it's right in front of them, they are searching other places to find it. The gold is your newest person's circle of influence. It is there waiting for you to talk to, nurture, and start creating an awesome team.

Drive Your Lines

"CI" circle of influence. Know it. Know how to tap into it and use it quickly. You have two weeks! The next part of the equation, "DL", stands for driving lines.

We need to be driving lines, finding leaders, and mining that gold. When I say driving lines, I mean that you need to be helping your newest leader tap into their circle of influence and start making connections. The more people they connect with the easier it will be to find the next level teams that you can drive the line with, because we are going to do the exact same thing with their circle of influence. We do this by quickly getting into their circle of influence for two main reasons. The first reason is to help them see success; these are warm contacts. They are going to have a better chance of not only getting people to join them, but keeping people in the business because there`s already a personal relationship of trust. It`s the fastest and most effective way to move.

Not only do we want to help our people get their business started by getting into their circle of influence and giving them wins, but there`s another reason you need to get into their circle of influence as fast as you can. The second reason is to ensure that the time you are investing into working and training them isn`t wasted or in vain. You don`t have time to waste.

You don`t know what`s going to happen. Unfortunately, some people quit and don`t have the stick-to-itiveness needed or the long-term vision. Some aren`t going to be consistent long enough to be able to make something happen. If you spend time investing in them but don`t get into their circle of influence, and they do end up quitting.

The time spent teaching and training them is wasted. If you got into their circle of influence and are driving that line, then even if they do quit you didn`t waste your time.

It`s important to remember the saying, "you go wide for show and deep for dough". If you want to make real money and create long term residual income, you have to drive lines. It`s not just about how many people you personally sponsor, it`s about how deep you can drive that line from circle of influence to circle of influence.

Driving lines are needed to create depth, but that`s not the end goal. So, what is the purpose for driving lines? What are you trying to accomplish? This is where the next part of the equation comes in. The next two "Ls" stand for lock legs. We are driving lines and now we are locking legs.

What does it mean to lock a leg? It means you drive that depth through circles of influence until you find that leader that is better than all of us. It could be two levels deep, it could be eight levels deep. I don`t care how many levels deep it is. You drive it until you find that leader. This person is called "the locker." This is the person that is on fire, and they will succeed in this business. They are willing to work, have a desire to succeed, and would do this business with or without you. Once you find the locker you work with them; camp on them for a couple of months to help them solidify their own team.

When you start mentoring "the locker," you not only help them, but you help everyone above them. You also motivate everyone upline to get to work so that they can capitalize more from commission off of the volume that is now underneath them.

By doing this, two different scenarios can happen to those upline. The first scenario is what I mentioned above. I sponsored somebody, got into their circle of influence, and drove that line. This motivated everybody to go out, do more, and everyone works to hit the higher ranks. There is a second scenario that can also happen.

For example, once when I went and opened up a new country, I started with one individual who had seen some small success in networking. He had never done anything really big. I started working with him and got into his circle of influence. We found some people that saw the vision and wanted to build the opportunity.

I took that next person, got into their circle of influence, and started to drive that line. I did this and drove down until the fifth level. That is where I found the locker. He was committed, hardworking, passionate, and he wanted to make a difference. He wanted to change his life, and he was sick of being stuck in this situation he was in. So he was motivated.

What ended up happening is everybody above him lacked vision, weren`t coachable nor consistent, and over time they quit. Now that individual locker is at the top level of the company and is a millionaire.

Now I`m sure all those people that quit wish they would have stayed. They could have made a lot of money because of what happened had they stuck it out. Making the decision to quit hurt them, but it didn`t hurt me. Why? Because I drove the business and found my locker. Had I not done that, all the time I would have put into teaching, training, and supporting would have been wasted.

I was able to find somebody who ended up building a huge organization and became a multimillionaire. All because I understand and follow this equation. I find the circle of influence, I drive the lines, and lock the legs with the locker. I saw the first person I brought in as a circle of influence, and then I was willing to drive that line until I locked that leg.

Once you know and use the equation, you just start to repeat it with anyone that you have sponsored. This has happened to me so many times. The top money earned in my company now is not the person who was originally sponsored but was four levels deep. The three people above her quit, yet she went on to make millions of dollars. If I had not followed this equation, my time would have been wasted there as well.

If you don`t lock legs, then you have started something that you haven`t finished. It`s still undone. If you don`t lock legs, in most cases the whole team will slowly disintegrate and disappear. Even outside of this industry, how many times have you seen somebody halfway do something? They start something but don`t finish. What ends up happening to that project? Nothing! What happens is that dream never turns into reality. You must follow the equation.

Don`t just start a team; finish the team. Follow the equation. Circle of Influence +Driving Lines +Locking Legs= SO.

If you don`t do this, you will most likely still have some people continue to take the product or remain customers. But there was so much more potential, and you could have helped them in such a bigger capacity; you could have multiplied your personal time, energy, and effort spent.

Rinse And Repeat

L istening to this somebody might think, "So, is this management mode? Am I just managing my team?" Absolutely not! Remember what I said. You need to be driving lines. You`re not just working with people who you personally sponsor saying, "bring me more people, bring me more people."

You`re getting into their circle of influence, finding somebody to work with, and continuing that until you have locked and solidified that leg. You`re not managing your driving, you`re building. Once you`ve locked that leg, it`s time to sponsor or focus on another leg and do it again.

Now when you go focus on another team, you know that the previous leg is secure; it`s not going to disintegrate. You`re not spinning plates with all these teams trying to focus on helping every single person. You are helping and mentoring the people that are part of the equation for your business right now, as long as you have people willing to work and finish what you started. If you are unable to help someone get into their circle of influence, then move on.

You can`t halfway start a new team. You have to tie it down. You have to lock it in. Every once in a while this may just happen on its own. Don`t leave your team`s success up to chance. You must be willing to work, do the equation, and teach the equation to your team. When you can understand what needs to happen and how it needs to happen, you start to build just a little bit differently. The amazing thing is that your outcome will be totally different.

One of the things that I like to do is break it down to the ridiculous. I like to make it so clear and so apparent that it almost seems ridiculous. Now when you're seeing people as a circle of influence, you're driving lines and locking legs. As this is duplicated, let me show you an example of what can happen.

Let's say somebody has a list of people. Out of that list there are a hundred people that they can get a hold of and put through their company's system.

Out of those hundred people, let's say ten percent of them (ten people) decide to do something. If this duplication continues and they can each put their lists together, and get one hundred people each to go through this same process, that's one thousand people now being exposed to the system. If 10 percent of them do something and duplicate, now we have ten thousand people going through the system.

If duplication like this is happening because you are helping them get into their own circles of influence, how do you ever run out of people to talk to. When people tell me that they have run out of people to talk to, my first thought is, "How can you run out of people?" I know that they are not building through circles of influence and following this equation.

I have hundreds of thousands of people in my company in over forty-five countries. Now, if I were to send out a message and tell everyone, "If you have anybody that needs third party validation, or if you have anyone that you would like me to talk to about our products and opportunity, I'm available." Do you think I'd ever run out of people to talk to? I wouldn't have enough time in the day to talk to everyone! That is because of this equation. I didn't just sell directly to people, I networked and duplicated.

If you duplicate things right in your business, you can experience the same thing. Let me break it down for you into actionable steps to take right now.

Step 1. List how many active legs you have right now in your organization.

Step 2. Next, evaluate if there is duplication happening and whether or not that leg is locked with a solid leader.

Step 3. Find the legs that aren`t locked, and launch or relaunch these teams.

Step 4. Drive the business as deep as it takes to find the locker and lock that leg.

If you want to speed up your results and see success faster, then your approach has to be intentional. You have to have a purpose. You have to have a plan. You have to know what your strategy is and what you`re going to accomplish.

When I understood the principles and implemented this equation into my team and my business, we went from doing hundreds of thousands of dollars in sales to hundreds of millions of dollars in sales.

This industry is a platform that can not only change your life but can change so many other people`s lives in the process. You can make a difference and be the difference in someone else`s life.

Multiply your time, energy, and effort by doing the right activities. Build a business intentionally and by design. Create insurance for your future by building a solid organization.

You`re in the right place. You have what it takes. It`s time to go make it happen. What the world needs right now more than ever is leadership. It`s time to rise to the occasion and grow into your greatness. I hope this chapter is something that can help you make a difference in your business and in your future. I wish you continued success because you deserve it.

This is the best time in the world to have the opportunity to be in this industry. You are empowering people. The world needs us more than ever. This industry will continue to thrive. What we have is better and better always wins.

Go look at your teams. See what you need to lock into place. When you have the newest person start, drive down and see what you can find. Utilize them and help them create a legacy. Teach others how to do this. Drive them to the center of the earth. Find the leader that is better than any of us because they are out there. If you do that and lock your organization in, you will build a solid business. Be *that* person. Be the person that changes generations to come because you put in the time, energy, and effort when it mattered.

Coaches Notes: These are some of the most advanced strategies in all of network marketing. Be patient. They take time to execute. Come back and study this chapter over and over. Take your own assessment on where you are strong and where you need work. As Stephen Covey says, "Begin with the end in mind." These strategies give you a vision of where you want to be. These strategies give you focus on some of the most advanced techniques in all of network marketing.

Author: Michele Calello

- Team ranked number six companywide in sales for 2019-2020.
- Six figure monthly earner.
- Top rank in the company.

"If you can look your why in the face and say, 'You're no longer reason enough;' then you can quit."

I started network marketing as a new mother at the age of twenty-two. I was not a good salesperson. I was actually terrible. I hated talking to people and was so shy. I don`t know how I got into sales, but I knew that it could be helpful for my family and help make ends meet. I was desperate to make ends meet.

There was money missing all of the time, and I later found out that was due to my ex buying drugs and not working when he said he was working. He told me work was being done. It was an abusive relationship that I didn`t tell anyone about because I was terrified all of the time, and quite frankly I was embarrassed. It was a terrible time in my life. Network marketing was an escape for me. It was an escape from the nightmare I was living.

Years later, I had gotten a divorce and was a single mom to two kids. I had jumped around to a lot of different companies. I was a company jumper. I didn`t find success until ten years in. I am going to say that again because it is important. I didn`t find success until ten years into network marketing.

I didn`t quit. I found my groove and found what I was looking for this whole time, including a real relationship built on love and trust. I just retired; my now husband of ten years retired from his job. We have five kids, and we are home for all of the fun and madness together. We can pick up and go at any time. None of that would have happened without network marketing.

Here is the thing that I don`t think people in our business talk about enough. I had to fall flat on my face multiple times. I have had people yell at me for contacting them. People have unfriended me. The biggest thing was to not listen and keep plugging along. I kept thinking, "They don`t pay my bills." I kept wondering what was keeping me from success. I had to do things the wrong way and figure them out.

Coaches Notes: Michelle is another reminder that sometimes our greatest perceived weakness is actually our hidden strength. Let me explain. Michelle, like me, felt she was naturally shy and not great at sales. This limiting belief made her feel that network marketing was never really a good fit. She later learned that this perceived weakness made her more relatable and was a massive strength. Don`t allow yourself to believe that you are not good enough. I have traveled and spoken to teams all over the world. Someone out there with a skillset much less than yours, and a region much tougher than yours, has done ten times more than you. This isn`t to put you down. This is to empower what you can do. I have seen every walk of life and background have success in this incredible profession. Yes, you can do it. Yes, it does begin with mindset.

Learn It All

That is why I always say that you need to be ready to learn. You must be looking for people who have made it to see what they are doing. It kills me when people say they are trying their hardest and it is not working. I always tell people I tried what I thought was my hardest too for ten years. I didn`t realize that I was capable of so much more. You have to stick to it and vow to never give up. Most people quit before they even give themselves an opportunity to learn and figure out all the processes.

Be a "learn it all." Always see what people are doing and keep learning. What works for one person may not work for another. Figure out your niche and see what will happen. Let me repeat. NEVER. GIVE. UP. If I had given up one, four, even six years in, you`d probably find me making peanuts as an elementary school teacher and NOT living the life with my family that I am living today.

What really spoke to me as I was "learning it all" was that when you are recruiting quality recruits, recruiting quality is much better than quantity. You can recruit everyone until you are blue in the face. If you continue to coach the people that are "time suckers`` and just want all of your attention, they will keep asking the questions and not utilizing what you say. Recruit people that have drive. Let people know up front that it doesn`t matter how long it takes you as long as you`re ready to learn, take advice, and run. This could be something huge for them if they are ready.

Let people come in, and set the expectation that it is going to take work if their goals and dreams are to become dependent on their company for living expenses. There are people that will come in and just want to make a car payment. That is ok! Never project your own goals onto other people. Meet them where they are at, but let them know they are going to have to work HARD if they have set BIG GOALS. If their goals aren`t to make the big bucks, still help them but don`t spend so much time with them that you lose time with the big hitters. ALL types of enrollments are important, but it`s also important to maximize your own time wisely.

Find The Big Goals

If your goal is to reach the top of the company. Don`t spend a lot of time on people that don`t have goals. You can recruit everyone, but spend your time with people who are ready to run. It may sound harsh, but it isn`t. You want to make sure that you are hitting the goal that you have set for yourself as well.

The first thing you should do is ask them what their goals are. Are they just wanting a car payment, or are they wanting to make a successful career out of this. Work with the people that want to be worked with and let the others do their thing! Sometimes, people just want the community and don`t want you breathing down their neck.

Find the people with the big goals. Everyone is welcome. This is why I always say to recruit quality over quantity, because your time is valuable. Make sure your time is well spent.

Here is a strategy that can help you find quality. From the very start, ask your prospect questions. Take a moment and ask, "What would your goals be if you join this company?"

Goals can change, but you want to see where they are at. How do they fit in your business? If their very first goal is to make this a business, then you can show them what it looks like. Help them make the commitment whatever it looks like. Ask them, "What can you set aside each week to focus on your business?"

This is also going to help you know where they are at with the right mindset of what it looks like to grow a business. Network Marketing is simple. The processes are simple. And for most companies, they are the same. But it won`t always be EASY. Sometimes, you have to do HARD THINGS no matter how simple they are. Such as getting out of your own head and asking the questions to get the sale or recruit. Your recruits should know that from the start. Don`t ever tell them that it`s going to be EASY and they hardly need to do anything. You`re setting yourself up to have a team of lazy recruits if you do this!

Want to find out who your true runners are going to be? Find a book about the business that you love and ask them to read it. Doesn`t even matter what book it is. (Rob`s books are great to start with ... hint hint) If they read that book, they may be your runners. This can be the first step to see their commitment level to the business. Tell them you will be checking in on them to see what they thought. It is like a test to see if they are going to be your runners. You can always help people make extra money, but they may not be the person that you are running and checking in with every day. This again is why one of the very first questions you ask should be, "What are your goals in this business?"

I am very competitive. I always look at the company leaderboards and want to be there. But when it comes to the monthly amount of recruits, I have to step back and remind myself that it isn`t always about the leaderboard. I have built a very successful business, running a massive team of over 25,000, and I have been on the top monthly recruiting leaderboard maybe once. My goal can be to recruit 2-3 people a month and I can still build massive success. When I have 2-3 people to work with a month, it helps keep me sane and be able to focus on their success. I can onboard them successfully and really invest in their success. It also gives me time to be with my team and my personal business. Don`t stretch yourself too thin. You`ll burn out quickly and won`t be the best leader you can be!

Coaches Notes: I love how Michelle communicated this section. Questions are the answers. Everyone has a completely different dream and goal in life. This is why it is so key to become a professional at asking the right questions. What is it they really want? Are they wanting to make that car payment? Are they wanting to go on more family trips? Many times at the beginning they can`t think big enough, so you need to meet them where they are at. You will need to do as Michelle says and start with small commitments, stepping them into more and more as they progress.

Know How To Lead

Your personal business should never suffer because of your leadership. It is important to keep that in the forefront. You have to do the things that you are teaching your team to do. If you expect your team to do things, you should be doing them. You can have less recruits with more potential. I know that for me, personally, there is no way I can manage my time if I am bringing in 20 new recruits a month. I already have 5 kids with four of them school aged and being homeschooled (thanks Covid). We are a competitive soccer family, Taekwondo family, and honestly, each day is interesting with also having a 1 year old. I don`t have TIME to successfully train 20 people! That`s life!

When you start out and build your new team, look at who you are wanting to run with. Never make the decision for people. Everyone has potential, but just really think about who you want to run with. Let new people know that your time is valuable. You and your upline should have processes in place which make training uniformed and easier. Make sure it is people that won`t waste your time. When you are new, you are still learning. Make sure you are still putting value on your own time. You don`t turn anyone away, but you make sure you decide how much time to spend on that person. People change all the time, and you can change with them, but be clear what your time is. Know where you want your time to be directed. Don`t spend time chasing people who say they want success but don`t follow your direction in doing so.

I have personally never felt much confidence in my life and my decisions before these last few years. I could never stand up in front of a room. I dropped out of college because they wanted me to take public speaking and stand in front of a room and give a speech. I couldn`t do it. I am now able to stand in front of thousands of people and have confidence in what I am saying and doing. Network marketing gave me that. Training myself to do hard things gave me that. Do I still have sweaty palms before a big speech? Yes. Do I still sometimes wonder if my processes are correct and could they be better? Yes. Always. It`s important to not get complacent and to KEEP LEARNING.

Something that I see people have the biggest struggles with is recruiting. It is the biggest thing people think there is a secret to. There isn`t. It comes down to asking people to do this business. If you see someone you want to work with, ask them. I will tell people that they are on my list. It helps break the ice and let people know that you are interested in them. Don`t make things weird, make them personal. Don`t be a spam bot; that is gross. Talk to the humans and don`t make them feel like a number. People get stuck on asking the questions. I am a socially awkward person. If I break the ice and tell people I am nervous to ask something, but I am going to do it anyway, it breaks the ice. Guess what? Most people are the same! They respect your honesty. Don`t make it weird. Just come out and be normal. I just tell people I think they would be awesome at what I do. I tell them if they aren`t interested, no big deal.

You are going to have insecurities and doubts, but you can do this. I have recruiting blitzes with people on my team. It is a ton of fun. How many people can you contact? How many people can you get to look at the business? When I realized all I had to do was talk to people like humans it made all the difference. Don`t be a spammy sammy. Just talk to people. It sounds easier than it is. I get it. Just get into the right frame of mind. I wanted to share this because I had to learn how to do it first before I led a team and showed them how to do it. For a good six to seven years, I was doing it all wrong. Be the leader of your team. Put yourself out there even when you have doubts and insecurities.

It Will Change Your Life If You Let It

When we started with this company, we were on the brink of foreclosure. I had failed at another business and we were going to lose our home. We have been with this company for three years, and we have been able to not only catch up on the house payments of the house we almost foreclosed on, but we just paid it off and have renters living in it.

We rented that house out and moved into another house that suits our family of seven better. A beautiful big house that has a waterway that leads out to the Gulf of Mexico. I don`t say this to brag. I say this because YOU CAN MAKE YOUR DREAMS COME TRUE TOO. My husband has retired from work because it didn`t make sense to have him away from our family any longer. He is now home helping raise our kids. It has completely changed our lives. My advice to everyone is to not give up. Can you imagine me giving up five years ago. You may not have all of the right answers. That is ok. I invest in myself and I will always be learning. I invest in coaching with Rob and other people. It is huge.

It is important to share the trials as well. I am being asked to be a part of this book. The people that are successful in this book and in your company are average people just like you. My first husband was buying drugs and stealing money from me while I was trying to make ends meet. I did write bad checks to the grocery store just to get food. We got evicted and had both of our cars repossessed. If you can see that you don`t have to live like that forever, that is huge.

My husband of ten years and I got pregnant before my divorce was final. I share that because it is real. I have done shady things to get by. It is ok. It doesn`t have to be your life forever. I always tell my team to be a real person. Show people your life, or what it used to look like. The biggest part of recruiting is being relatable. A real person went from foreclosure to a millionaire. I was one of my company`s first millionaires. How amazing is that?!

Your life right now doesn`t have to be your life forever. I believe that. I have lived that. I want that for you too. Don`t give up on yourself. Create the life that is your dream.

Coaches Notes: The greatest investments you will ever make are in yourself and your relationships. These days we can`t rely on a degree or job security. Our best insurance policy is investing into ourselves and our relationships. You are discovering more and more insights, from different leaders, on how they accomplished success. Each one of them has a different story. Each one of them had doubts. One of the hardest parts about network marketing is not knowing WHEN it will happen. If you knew it would take five years that would be longer than you had hoped, but it would be worth it to create financial freedom. The fact you just don`t know, many people quit because they want certainty. Here is a huge tip to help you along the way, any time a negative thought comes to your mind, write down three solutions immediately. This strategy will literally change your life. It will train and retrain your brain to work for you rather than against you. Eventually, you will focus 90 percent or more of your time on solutions rather than problems.

Author: Amanda Call

- Wife of 17 years, mother of 3 children, and 18 year flight attendant
- Grew current company by over 300%
- Created a social selling funnel with over 30,000 customers
- Multimillion dollar team sales in first nine months
- Top 3 leader in company
- Helped create a hero product with a 6 hour launch sell out

"Build it and they will come" only works in the movies. Social Media is a "build it, nurture it, and engage them, and they may come and stay."

-Seth Godin

I want to be crystal clear on a misconception many have about Network Marketing. EVERYONE can win. EVERYONE can be successful. It is simply a choice. I joined my current company earlier this year. Since then, my team has increased the size of the company by over 300% and increased sales by even more than that. There are new leaders every single month. If you believe in network marketing, you believe in your products, and you make the decision to be successful you will be.

I wasn`t looking for network marketing. I wasn`t looking for a business. I was a super busy working mom with two-year-old twins and a four-year-old at home. I had a friend who was posting about a product that caught my eye. I finally went to her website and realized it was just a smart decision to buy the business kit.

That decision changed my life. I know that sounds dramatic, but it is the truth. It was the first time I had the vision of what network marketing could do. I was seeing it change the lives of others and knew that I could do that too.

It wasn`t just the money, even though that was a factor. I found confidence that I didn`t realize I had. I instantly felt connected with a large group of people and felt like I had a life outside of motherhood and work. It gave me an identity and goals, and that felt good!

Life outside of motherhood doesn`t have to mean you have to leave the house! You can build this business online and leverage your social media to build a business, create connections, and get to know new people.

In today`s world, we have to realize that a huge portion of our networking is done online .... and the vast majority of the networking we do online happens on social media. We have an endless network of people. Without our network, we would just be marketers and that makes me think of working a 40-50 hour work week in corporate America. No thank you!

We want to use social media to our advantage when building our business; I believe it is more crucial now than ever before. We have access to an endless network when using social media. We don`t even have to leave the comfort of our home to access millions and millions of new leads.

In network marketing, our entire business revolves around growing our network. When we leverage something, we use it to our advantage to get to where we want to be. Anyone who is taking the time to read a book on this business, apparently takes this business seriously. You see the value in this industry.

If you are just starting, you are probably cautiously optimistic. I am here to tell you the stories you hear of people being successful does not have to just be a pipe dream. Many start in with excuses shortly after they begin .... And one of the excuses we hear time and time again is that I don`t know enough people. THIS is why leveraging social media is vital to your business. You have an endless network of other people. If you truly believe in your product or service that your company offers, you know that people need it. If you believe in this industry, you realize that everyone needs to know about the opportunity to do this. You have a hunger to help as many people as possible and social media is the most effective way to reach the masses.

Smell You From A Mile Away

I think a big mistake that many people make is trying to create a persona or trying to become too much like someone else on social media. I don`t care what platform you are using ... inauthenticity can be smelled from a mile away. You have to be you.

I remember about a year into my network marketing career I was talking with my friend, Angie, about how I felt like I had plateaued. I wasn`t able to sponsor anyone, and I wasn`t getting the sales that I wanted. I was basically throwing myself a pity party. The conversation that followed is so crystal clear in my head because it was a game changer for me.

Angie asked me if I sponsored more people I met in real life or those that I met online. I told her that the majority were people I had known in real life at some point. She asked me how that was possible since our particular company relied so heavily on an online platform. I stopped and thought about it for a while.

I KNEW that a larger percentage of my social networking base I had met online, but a very teeny, tiny fraction of them had joined me in my NWM business. When I told her this, she said, "You are the most fun person to be around when we are together. Do you think that comes across online?"

All of a sudden, it hit me. I was trying to be what I thought someone successful in network marketing looks like and acts like instead of letting people see ME being successful in network marketing. I was trying to create the persona of whom I thought I should be instead of having the success fit who I was.

I had to take a step back and really realize what that meant. What are my best traits? What makes me me? Is who I am coming across in my posts, my messages, and in my comments on other people`s posts? The answer was no.

One of the best ways that I suggest for people to begin leveraging social media in their network marketing business is by using attraction marketing. It is a simple way to give snippets of what your business is doing in your life, in an indirect way.

No one wants to follow someone who is a billboard for a company. Social media allows you to build curiosity and show who you are, as a result of what you do, without having to blatantly say it. This is what attraction marketing is.

I don`t care if you are just starting out or if you are a seasoned veteran making seven figures. What you are doing with your business has impacted your life in one way or another. Think of attraction marketing as the long game. You want to draw interest to your brand and your lifestyle through authentic posts.

This looks different for every single person. A friend of mine described it as a way of "flirting" with your brand. Think about when you first met your significant other ... You didn`t lay it all out on the table to begin with, right? There was an act of subtlety to what you were doing, and it worked!

I hate, hate, hate cleaning my house. I am in no way a neat freak, but I also was raised to know that we should not let people into our house when it is a mess. I also am social by nature and want people to come to my house and visit. It is quite a conundrum. When I began my NWM business, I knew that one of my first big splurges would be to have someone clean my house. As a busy working mom with three young kids at home, it just made sense, but I had never been able to justify the expense before. You can bet when I started bringing home a paycheck big enough to cover a house cleaner, I definitely got one.

Here is the key to attraction marketing: you want to express how you no longer have a struggle due to your current circumstances while remaining humble about it. You always want to come from a place of gratitude and not arrogance or ego.

When I hired a housekeeper, it would be easy to post about how my new business was affording me the luxury of a housecleaner. But remember...the key is subtlety. People know you have a new business. They can put two and two together. You can just express gratitude for your new splurge that you have never given yourself before. Do you see the difference?

Billboard post: My new business just paid for my housecleaner!

Attraction marketing post: I am so grateful to have the extra time with my family that I would normally spend cleaning the house on a Saturday morning.

Billboard post: Look at my amazing manicure I got using my (insert company name) card.

Attraction Marketing post: Spoiling myself a couple times a month with a mani/pedi sure is a life I can easily get used to.

Can you see the difference? People know what you do. Don`t be a billboard for your company. Be an example of what your company can do for someone`s life.

Coaches Notes: Attraction marketing is something that very few get. I have the great privilege of personally coaching Amanda in my one on one coaching program, and I have seen firsthand her strategies. She has absolutely smashed it with focusing on not being a billboard while providing a ton of value. She is very deliberate in what she posts. She knows her exact target market and audience. My challenge for you is to begin to figure out WHO you want to attract in your business. What is the average age and gender? What type of person. For example, a leader just told me yesterday her goal was to focus on 30 to 40 year old moms who are in North America. She got much more specific than that but this at least gives you a starting point. When you know your target market you know exactly who your posts are speaking to.

Your First Online Task

When just starting out in network marketing, I think the biggest thing you can do on social media is to be present. Do not instantly start spamming your Facebook wall, Instagram, or whatever you use with your business. Build relationships. Start commenting on people`s stories and posts. If you see something you connect with in a post, send them a private message and let them know how you connected with it. Be interested in people`s lives.

If a lot of this sounds like the same sort of advice you got when reading *How to Win Friends and Influence People* by Dale Carnegie, it is because the principles in that book hold true regardless of your platform. If you have never read that book, it should be the first book you read as soon as you finish this one. We want to make others feel important and the best way to do that is to be interested in their life.

Of course, you need to post as well. This is where figuring out your branding becomes vital. You need to be a person that they see and whose life looks intriguing enough to make someone stop their scroll. You will need to do what works for you, but I recommend posting no less than one time a day when you start; you can even post up to three times per day. I know this might sound like a lot to some of you, but you have to remember that most people will not see everything you post. You are also going to make those posts be about a variety of things. Remember the three to five things that you found out from your network about what makes you, you? That is what you will be sharing. You won`t be making one to three posts a day about your business. Only about one out of every four posts should be about your business, and even those posts should be more about attraction marketing or curiosity seeking than blatant posts.

I know you might be thinking, if I am not blatantly posting about my business on my wall on FB or my feed on IG, how will people know what I am doing? You will be posting about it. People will become curious about what you do based on your attraction marketing and curiosity seeking posts. They will find out what you do.

The place where I am completely blatant with my business is in my stories. I still mix it up with humorous posts and things from my day to day life, but I will put sales that my company is having in my stories. I will put before and after situations using the products that we sell in my stories. I take more liberties in my stories because they are only going to last for 24 hours and I am mixing it with a number of other things. It just feels like an organic part of my life.

When starting out in Network Marketing, it is so easy to initially feel insecure. You start telling yourself a fake story ... no one wants what you have to offer, no one wants to join you, people are going to talk about you. None of these are true. You are letting your fear of judgment hold you back.

This is the joy of social media. It is so much easier to be brave from behind a computer screen (we see this every day with all the trolls out there, right?). Use the fearlessness you feel behind a screen to your advantage! No one is going to eat you. Seriously, think about the absolute worst-case scenario. What does that look like? Rob says that, "if you don`t have haters, you aren`t working hard enough". The worst-case scenario is that you have haters. Guess what? That means you are working hard! Good job, friend!!

My upline, who is my best friend, has taught me so many valuable things along the way, but I believe the most important thing she has taught me has been simply through her example. She could easily have haters. She is this confident, gorgeous woman who makes a killing at what she does. She has very, very few people who don`t just adore her, and do you want to know why? It is because she makes you feel like a million dollars when you are around her. She edifies everyone and makes them feel important, and she sincerely compliments them. So, if you are worried about people talking about you and judging you, just follow her lead. Make them feel like they are the bees` knees. It is hard to hate someone who is being so kind to you, right? And we have already talked that we are in the business of networking, which means building relationships, right? So just continue genuinely caring about people and making them feel important. When you see an opportunity to compliment them, take it! This can be done so easily on social media, so do it.

The Next Step

One of the biggest keys to being successful in network marketing is to talk to new people every day. This might sound daunting to many, but when you take social media into the equation you realize that this is actually an attainable goal.

You want to make five new contacts every single day. This doesn`t mean that you need to be best friends with five new people every day. It means becoming a part of their broad circle.

If I told you to go out every single day and meet five new people in person, you would quit today, right? We have learned that our circumstances can change in just a matter of a moment. We can use March 2020 as our proof of that. If anyone the previous year had told you that basically the whole world would shut down, only the most essential of businesses would be open, people wouldn`t be leaving their houses, vacations would be canceled, and there wouldn`t be any concerts, parties, or conventions, you would have thought that whoever told you that was crazy.

This is why it is vital to utilize social media. It not only connects you to new people, it helps you to remain close to those already in your circle. I do believe that you need to be calling, texting, and messaging people when you begin. But social media allows people to get to know you, your lifestyle, and your brand without you having to call them and tell them what it is. It is an organic way to let people into your life without forcing them to hear about it.

I see people who are just beginning in network marketing feel like they need to know everything immediately. They think if they read all the books, watch all the videos, and ask every question they will be guaranteed success. The problem is that by the time they are ready to finally begin, they have lost that initial excitement.

Just jump! Just do it. Ask questions along the way and learn what you can, but do not become a professional student. You will learn as you grow. It will happen organically.

Don`t be afraid to share your story and connect with people. It seems scary to go live on social media and tell your story, but you are the only one who can tell it. It is ok to be vulnerable. It is ok to fumble. That is what makes you real and relatable and makes others realize you don`t have to be perfect to do what you do.

Network Marketing has literally changed my entire life. My best friends are the ones I have met in this industry. The products that I sell are revolutionary. I have taken a long leave of absence from work. I am home with my children all the time. The vacations that we go on are a direct result of what I do. We have time freedom we have never had before.

I know my confidence stems directly from this business. I have found a passion for helping other women find that same confidence. It is amazing for this to be so life changing for my family and me, and to see the other women on my team be able to accomplish goals that they never thought possible is seriously the most fulfilling thing in the world. They are making both small and big dreams become realities. To see people be able to treat themselves to their housekeepers, pay for their children`s extracurriculars, get out of debt, pay their mortgage, and a million other things is what makes this worth all the time and effort.

Coaches Notes: Build relationships! Amanda hits on this hard because it is vital to your success. You are NOT SPAMELA PAMELA! I talk about this a lot in my book *The Game of Networking*. Your goal is to discover how to build quick relationships. Amanda gives you several insights on ways to do that. Simple ways such as commenting on others posts, using stories, and making regular posts. Every little bit helps to bridge the gap with others. It all adds up to building trust quickly. Talking to new people is the lifeblood of this business, which is why Amanda is adamant that you talk to NEW PEOPLE DAILY.

Social Media Changes Lives

The company I am currently with has been around for many years but had very few reps when I started. When I asked the CEO why this was, she told me that the girls who were there had been doing it forever and were predominantly doing home-based parties. They had not grown because they didn`t want to. They made great commissions just selling the product and believed that anyone they sponsored became immediate competition.

Of course, anyone reading this book knows this is not how the industry works, but it is a common belief with those who don`t see the abundance in network marketing. We also knew that we did not want to come in and do home parties. It was not our personal style and we wanted to go big with social media.

Fast forward just six months and we have increased the number of representatives by 700 percent .... Yes, you read that right; we have had a 700 percent increase in just six months because we leveraged social media. We found ways to market ourselves online and created amazing systems using social media. We didn`t have to have that scarcity mindset because we know that when using social media, there is always an abundance of people and a never-ending network. We don`t believe that other advisors are competition but are cohorts who help and support us.

Social media has completely transformed the business model for this company. It can completely transform your personal business, as well. I believe that absolutely. Social media is a game-changer, and it can be a game-changer for your life as well.

Coaches Notes: Social media is no longer the future ... it is the present. Discovering how to use social media the right way is a must for your business to thrive. Think of social media as the great enhancer. Done right, social media will help you find more warm leads and have more customers/business builders sign up. The concepts of social media are not complicated, but you will need to follow the plan Amanda laid out and then stick to that plan. Results don`t usually come right away, but keep the vision because they will happen.

Author: Alli Carlson

- One of the top ranks in her company.

- Started a "girl gang" of women aggressively supporting other women (AKA her team).

- Proud wife and mama.

- Successful podcast.

"I'm coming for everything they said I couldn't have."

I am so excited to be able to share about recruiting. I can't think of a better topic to learn about when you are first getting started in network marketing. Here's the best part: the more you learn, the more it helps your business throughout your journey. This business has many parts to it, but it really all comes down to recruiting.

Recruiting starts with work behind the scenes. Think about the first impression people are getting of you. Most of the time, it starts on social media with your profile. If you had a storefront that people were coming to, what does it look like? Is it inviting to customers? Do people know who you are and what you sell based on the storefront? If your storefront was a disaster or it was confusing to decide what you sold, you wouldn't get very many customers. In the virtual world, your storefront is your profile. What are you portraying yourself as? What are you posting about?

Positivity, authenticity, humor, and insightfulness are always going to draw people into you. People are drawn to things that click for them. They are looking for people that they can connect with. On the flip side of that, think about what detracts people from you. Maybe it is a post about your drama.

In the world we are living in right now, people have enough drama in their own lives. They don't need to have your drama, too. Thinking of things that are turn offs to people is important. Stop and think about what is attracting and detracting people from you.

Coaches Notes: At this exact moment, I have done 113 podcast episodes for "Network Marketing Breakthroughs with Rob Sperry." Currently, the episode Alli was in is ranked number three. Why? Because she knows her stuff. Recruiting is the number one most important aspect in network marketing. Without recruiting, there is no retention. Without recruiting, there is no culture to create.

Without recruiting, you have no business. Most distributors try to focus on everything but recruiting. Alli is going to hit recruiting head on in this section.

Recruiting starts on your profile, before it starts anywhere else. Start by looking at your profile and asking for feedback from others, to see what they think when they first see your profile.

Second, look at your posts. Posting is a process that you grow and develop over time. You can't just start posting today and get results tomorrow. In today's instant gratification climate, people think they can post one thing and it is going to be on fire. They think they won't have to do anything else in their business for the rest of the week because of their one post. It doesn't work that way. No matter where you are in your journey, you will be working the business!

If you had a traditional business in the beginning, no one else is going to show up, unlock the door, turn on the light, sort the clothes, or check on the inventory. You are the one that has to do that. There are certain necessary things in this business, and you are the one that has to do them in order to be successful. The sooner that you can adapt as the owner of this business, the more successful you will be. The difference is that employees only think about the work that has to be done. They just want to do what they have to do to get paid. An entrepreneur looks at things differently. They see it as a passion, an interest. They put into it what they want to see out of it. They create a legacy.

You have to start seeing yourself as an entrepreneur, and start posting from that mindset. Think about the difference between an entrepreneur and an employee. Only 4 percent of the population are entrepreneurs. The rest of the population are employees. You need to see that most people coming into your business are going to have an employee mindset. It is going to take some work to shift their mindset to work their business as an entrepreneur. One thing that I have done with my team is help them shift their social media to be more entrepreneur-minded than employee-minded. This is a strategy that I use to help them see how using social media can be the gateway to a successful business.

So often I hear people say, "Ok, I get I should use social media, but what do I post? What should I talk about? What does that look like?" I developed this concept called "branding fives."

You will have four different topics that you will talk about, and they are personal, product, compensation, and leadership. Within those four subjects, you will be branding five subjects that you want to post about. These are going to be subjects that you find you can post on over and over again. I have included examples below of what the branding five can look like in each category.

1) Personal five things you are going to post about–This should be your easiest category. Who are you? What are the five things that you want to talk about that are going to attract people to you? What is going to help people see you? What do you like? What are you good at?

   Here are my five–I`m a mom of four crazy humans. I am a wife. This helps people see that I am like them. I like to post funny things. I like to make people laugh. I tell stories about my kids driving me crazy and wanting to make me pull my weave out! I love to share the funny side of me because when I am in business mode, I am a boss. I love fashion and Amazon. I just had a conversation with my UPS guy because he is here every single day! My list is not going to be like any of your lists. I don`t know anything about sewing or cooking, but maybe you do. Think of the things that make you, you. Build the list for YOU!

2) Product five things you are going to post about–You should always know what you love about your products. Some people get so caught up in what to say. They want a script to see what to say to people. I always have to remind them about why they joined, and what they love about the products. This list should be the five things that brought you into this company. I love how our company is simple, quick, and easy. I love how delicious it is! The results are good. SEE?! Make it easy to post about why you love your product.

3) Compensation plan five things you are going to post about–A lot of people will say, "I don`t know how to get people on my team." When I go and look at their page, I wouldn`t know that they have an opportunity. If you believe in your comp plan, you need to tell people about it. We have something golden here. We need to be talking about it. Here are five things I would be talking about with a comp plan. Being paid every single week. Rank advance bonuses. No startup cost. Have a website with them. The relationship that you get to build.

4) Leadership five things you are going to post about–This can be about stepping up as a leader, or it can be about your team itself and how much you love them. Get creative here, because this is an opportunity to show people that you are leading a team! I dive into leadership when I don`t know where to start. I read books, listen to podcasts, and go to my favorite trainer. Post about that! People love to see what other people are reading or listening to, and it is a great engaging post.

Coaches Notes: "You have to start seeing yourself as an entrepreneur and start posting from that place. Think about the difference from an entrepreneur vs employee. Only 4 percent of the population are entrepreneurs. The rest of the population are employees." This part should shift everything for you. Your strategy on social media needs to be from a place that you are the creator of your business. You are attracting what you want to attract. Alli gave you four strategies to help you never run out of content to post. Take all of these strategies and create notes in your phone or in a notebook. Start to jot down ideas based on these strategies to generate content. Then continually do this on a weekly basis to help you improve your content, attraction marketing, and recruiting. It must be part of your DMOs. Want to learn more? Check out www.sperrybonus.com

The branding five can help the newest person start to see how easy it is to post. Some people say they won`t know what to post, but this guideline helps make it easy for people to go through and follow so they never run out of things to post and talk about to their audience.

I also get asked all of the time about the timing of posting. Now we are going to talk about when to post. Listen, it isn`t a timing problem that most people are having. You can post at any time of the day and get engagement. Most people don`t have a talent problem or can`t do it. What they have is consistency, work ethic, and worth problems. Don`t worry about timing, worry about consistency. Are you committed to being consistent with posting?

The amount of time you spend on the business is going to be different for everyone. This is a numbers game and you need to play the numbers. Some of those numbers include the number of hours you work on the business. The consistency is what matters most.

Consistency is one area that helps you in other areas of the business, as well. I have been the type of person that hasn`t done anything for the whole month and when the 25th hits, I go hard and go and enroll people. What would that month have looked like if I would have started the month off like that and continued to be consistent?

There aren`t bad months, there is bad consistency. Consistency boils down to the daily method of operation. Every single business has one. DMO just means what you do every single day. There are important things that need to be done every single day. Write out the different things you could or should be doing for your business. Put a star next to the five to seven things that you deem the most income producing or the most important for your business. Do those things every single day. There is a set of things that have to get done every single day. Just do them.

Customers can only come from conversations. Conversations, like posting, should be on your DMO. Recruiting starts way back with posting, but the only way you are going to get customers is by having conversations. Be smart about it. Act like you know what you are talking about. Build an actual relationship with them. You don`t want to just throw a product down people`s throats and leave. Respond to your customers in a timely manner. There are people out there that are not responding to their customers in a timely manner. People are used to quick responses in the climate we are in. They aren`t willing to wait around for people to get back to them. They will go and find people that will give them instant information and gratification.

If you ordered a cheeseburger right now, but you aren`t going to get it for seven days, you would just go somewhere else. Same thing with your customers. Get them while they are hot!

How many people can you get information to in an hour? How many can you consistently get information to in a day? The main thing here is figuring out how many people, at a bare minimum, you can put yourself in front of.

Where do you find people to have conversations with? I have a different spin on it. You all know friends, family, and co-workers. There are also nurses, teachers, doctors, influencers,and social media friends. Accept and understand that the people on this list are probably not going to be the one that is the rockstar. However, they know the one! Someone knows the one! They are important for the new people to get the initial sale and get your business up and running.

When people post things on Facebook, I like to do something called "permission marketing." When you are scrolling on Facebook, you find yourself just doing the scroll mindlessly. Sometimes our brain just has to shut off, but we can still use that time to build our businesses. You have seen people post about their pains. There is an opportunity here if you open your mind to it. Be on the lookout for those posts. You can use permission marketing. "Hey Amanda, I am so sorry you are experiencing that. I just sent you something in your DM to help you with that." Then you go into the DM and say, "Tell me more about ...." Ask people what they need, and they will tell you.

If you just tell them what your solution is and not ask them questions, that is completely different than asking and listening to what they have to say. You can then go into what you have as a solution.

How many of you are asking for referrals? This is another way of doing referral marketing, and it works great online and offline. Referrals are the way to get into a cold market. You have to ask friends, family, and co-workers. You have to ask! I want to challenge you to ask for the referral right after the sale. There isn`t going to be a time that this person is more excited than the moment they hit the submit button. They won`t ever match that excitement. It is that moment that you want to ask for the referral. Ask right then!

Be on the lookout for people that you can help with the business. There are people in the world that are begging for and needing the thing that you are offering. You need to take this responsibility very seriously. It sounds dramatic, but you have something that will change people's lives, and they need it and are begging for what you have to offer. Don't be the person that withholds that from people.

One of the mantras I say to myself that has kept me going, to succeed in this business is, "It is not over til it's over." I want to challenge you to not make it over til it's over. Now is not the time to slow down. Now is not the time to write off this year. Now it is time to show up and work. Use this book and the things you are being taught to go back in and make your business successful. Use the tools like "branding five" and see how you can incorporate them today to set yourself up for consistency, which ultimately will bring you success. Because really, it's not over til it's over.

> **Coaches Notes:** As Alli said, all of these great strategies mean absolutely nothing if you aren't consistent with them. You need to get focused. Being an entrepreneur is both rewarding and difficult. In a job, you are used to trading time for money. So many times, network marketers confuse being productive with being busy. If you head to www.sperrybonus.com, I will give you a downloadable infographic on my top income producing activities to keep you focused.

Author: Amber Deloof

- One of three people to hold her current rank in her company.

- Her team sells more than ten million dollars annually.

- She`s been a multiple six figure earner since 2013.

- Volunteer firefighter wife, a homeschooling mom of three elementary kids, an adoptive mom, and has a goal every summer to sleep in her RV more than her home.

- When she isn`t leading a team of thousands, you can find her on a couch with one or both of her mini schnauzers and a book.

"You can't give away millions unless you make millions."

Everything I've built in this industry has been built by being a human and keeping it simple. I can't tell you that I have built all of the systems, because that couldn't be further from the truth. But there are a few key things that I have done to build a very successful business, while traveling and camping with our family for the majority of our time.

YOUR FRIEND'S FRIENDS

When I got started in network marketing, I had ZERO clue what I was doing. Honestly, after I enrolled I wondered if maybe my husband was right and I had been scammed. All I truly knew was I couldn't dare let him be right, and I was going to prove him wrong. I had basically no network, but I was determined. I knew my family and friends, and I knew they had family and friends. I knew that if I wanted to create network marketing success that I would need to find more friends. It really is that simple. Find new friends. They are everywhere.

Facebook was still new back then (yikes, that makes me sound old!), so the first thing I did when I started in network marketing was I started tackling expanding my friends list and making friends. Not just adding them. This is HUGE, so I am going to say it again. Don't just hit the add button. I spent time on Facebook getting to know people. I was commenting and engaging with them. Do you know your FB friends' dog's names? I do. My FB friends list isn't a cold market. I've worked incredibly hard to cultivate that list into a warm market. You have to focus on doing the same thing. Start expanding your friends list. Get to know who your friends and family know.

People always ask me, "but how?" Remember, it`s simple. Let me give you an example. If my sister had a post up and someone posted a comment that was sarcastic and funny, I`d drop them a friend request. When they`d accept, I`d pop in messenger and say, "Hey! Thanks for accepting my request. You have my sarcastic humor and it felt like a good fit!" Sounds simple right? It is, but it`s also the one thing that I see so many people miss. Hit the add button, and then you need to actually connect.

When people start network marketing, they try to overcomplicate the process and they make getting more friends even harder and complex. Keep it simple. Get to know your friends and your family`s friends. Make authentic connections with people that you would want to get to know in real life.

So now that you have an expanded friends list, how are you going to sell to them? Keep in mind, I`ve never friended these people to hard sell them. I just wanted to make more friends. Many people have 5000 friends on Facebook and 3000 of them are cold market, meaning that they don`t even know them. Not me, I have 5000 people on Facebook that are my actual pool of friends. That is what we call a warm market! Warm markets are people that know me. We have things in common.

 One thing that I think is important to say is you can`t just make a few friends and expect to make sales. You need to create trust. You want your friends to know you, respect you, and root for you. Some people think that I overshare my life on social media, but I believe that transparency leads to trust. People want to engage with people that are being real and authentic, and sometimes that includes the overshare. If I have a hard day with my kids, my network knows it. If I struggle with motivation or something else, my network knows it. If I need accountability, they`re going to know it! What do I mean by overshare? I mean ... I SHARE! I even once did a live on a feminine care product. Listen, my friends needed to know about it, and I am here to share it! No matter how utterly humiliating it may be to people like my husband (and it was, HA!). Now, while I am a self-proclaimed oversharer, that doesn't include oversharing your product and opportunity! Building trust is important. Showing them different ways that you can help them and support them is important, but you can't just add someone as a friend and then get spammy on them.

I came from a company that spammed a lot. That is how we got trained and what we taught. Many people still do this, but it has hurt the industry as a whole and made it tricky for everyone. It also causes an adverse effect when we tell people not do it because then they don't know what to do. It's a darned if you do, darned if you don't kind of situation! They don't know how to market appropriately and they don't know how to offer appropriately, so they just end up doing nothing. That is not what we want for you and your business! We want you to connect and create a network that loves you and trusts that what you are doing is legit. So, from a recovering Spamela Anderson, I'd like to tell you that you can stop spamming and be a better marketer! I promise you can learn the ways of attraction marketing. If I can escape spammy marketing, so can you! I came out of the gates spamming my little face off! I realized after a while that this wasn't what it was supposed to be about, but at the time I wasn't that concerned about the process. I had one reason and one reason only to do it. MONEY. We were living from paycheck to three days before paycheck. Some months we couldn't even pay cash for our groceries. We were newlyweds and we just couldn't see any way to get ahead of this ongoing cycle. I dreamed of being able to pay cash for Christmas and vacations, but honestly, I would have loved to just pay cash for gas and groceries. So I thought being spammy was the only option to do this business. I just didn't see how simple it could have been.

Here is what had to happen for me. I had to stop listening to the static. I had to stop listening to the people who encouraged me to copy and paste posts and spam. It never felt right to me. It always felt gross to me. I stopped doing what others were doing, and I started being ME on social media. I joke that I was doing the whole attraction marketing thing before it was cool. I began to share my journey. I opened up about my struggles. And guess what? People started reaching out to me ... THANKING ME for being so open. People started to feel less alone. Of course, there were some people who told me I overshared. Those same people never supported me and would have never done business with me anyway, so I paid them no mind. At this point, I feel like if you are in network marketing and someone hasn`t complained that you overshare on Facebook, then you`re not sharing enough of yourself with your followers. You want it to be like you are talking to your best friend on the phone and letting them know about your day. Not the fake day that is a couple of well curated photos and Pinterest quotes, but the real day. You know the one! That day where you put yourself in a timeout in the closet and had to do a Facebook live quietly so that the kids don`t find you. Or the kind of day where you took your kid to gymnastics and realized in the parking lot that you still have your slippers on. Or you know what? Maybe you got back on track with workouts–SHARE IT! #gymselfieoritdidnthappen

It isn`t just about sharing the madness that is your life. You also have to give your network a reason to come back to your page regularly! I love to give value freely and not ask for anything in return. That is another way to build trust with your audience of friends. I have five umbrellas in my personal brand. I use these umbrellas to help me stay on track with what to share. Everyone`s umbrellas are different, but mine are: Family (homeschool life, adoption, car seat safety, marriage); Adventure (travel, camping, Jeeping); Influencer (motivation, inspiration); Health (exercise, diet, supplements), and Humor. I am sarcastic by nature. Humor and sass is a huge part of my brand. When I post, it has to fall under these umbrellas.

All of this is to say that my network knows me, knows my kids, and knows my mini schnauzers. They know I am an adoptive mom and that I homeschool. They know I`m a bookworm who loves Jeeps and traveling in my RV. They know I run a business online. I share about all of this and more.

They know me.

Make your network know you! Not the network marketing vision of you that someone else created.

> **Coaches Notes:** Niches to riches. You will hear me mention this several times throughout the book because this concept can change your business. Amber is one of the most real people I know. If you follow her on social media for a few months you will feel like you know her very well, without ever having met her. She has identified her umbrellas to talk about on social media and she is very deliberate on only focusing on those five themes. Your top goal on social media is CONNECTIONS. To fully master social media, you want people who have never met you to feel like they know you. This creates massive leverage. This helps you attract the right customers and business builders. Go start creating your umbrellas now so that you can have more FOCUS on social media.

The Value Of The Group

One of the things that helped me the most was finding my people. I had to find groups of people that care about the same things I care about. I had to find the people that like the same things I like.

Anyone who knows me, knows what I am into and what I spend my time doing. It`s crazy. I have built a following because of my book recommendations. Seriously! Reading super twisted psychological thrillers helped expand my following. I know! I am as shocked as you are that people actually care about what books I read! Book recommendations have helped me build my friend list, and total bonus ... I get to read and talk to people about great books! Find the things that interest you and that will connect to others with the same interests.

It is always about being friends first, and if business comes it will come. Focus on what makes you tick and join groups around that. I own a Peloton, so I am in a Peloton group. I am in a Peloton book group for moms! YES! That is actually a thing. Get out and join groups of people that are like you. Then you aren`t cold messaging people. You are talking about books, parenting, accountability, etc. They become REAL friends. Make actual connections and that will grow your list.

If you haven`t started looking into groups on Facebook, let me tell you something, there is a group for everything out there. I mean everything. You can find your Peloton mom book group or whatever else you are into. Like knitting? There is a group! Homeschooling? A million groups! Do you own a certain breed of dog? There is a group for you! You can find groups and join them. But that`s just the first step.

You have to engage in those groups. Here is a simple system for groups. Join groups, add posts, and engage on other people`s posts. Then go back to your own page and add value there. If people like you in the group, they will search for you outside of the group and start following you. Simple!

Value posts can be anything. Think about what can help someone today. Post on your personal page about how great your Peloton group is and what goals you are hoping to find there. Listen, keep it simple! Once, I found a Chipotle hack to save people 400 calories without losing anything! You can bet I shared that! People truly overthink this! A quick tip about how to get in more steps! Tips for getting in more water! Heck, can you fold fitted sheets like a magician? Share that ... then send me the video so I can learn! Post about how your product is helping others or what you and your team have been up to. But keep this to once every five or so posts! It can be anything that is going to make someone stop and want to see what you are up to.

In 2016, we adopted a child from China to complete our family. She was 21 months old and has a super rare genetic disorder. I found a group on Facebook that has other families with children with this genetic disorder. It was important for me to be there, not only because I needed education and support for my daughter, but because international adoptive moms understood my journey in a way that not many could. We built friendships and helped others.

Through doing this, I built great friendships, and several are already in network marketing. I met one that joined my team, and multiple adoptive moms joined our team. We became known for having adoptive families on our team. It is now one of the biggest legs on our team because it is all about community. Also, sharing our adoption experience touched a ton of people, and it truly grew and scaled our business because we were being transparent about our experience. It helped to take my business to what I have always dreamed it could become.

Coaches Notes: This is one of the best strategies I have ever seen for never running out of warm leads. Too many people make it complicated and join groups that fit their business. For example: if your company focuses on weight loss, don`t go find weight loss Facebook groups. You have it all backwards. Follow Amber`s strategy of finding Facebook interest groups. What are you passionate about? Now go and find those groups and interact there. Why? Because these are people you have something in common with. It won`t feel like fake chit chat. Of course you want them to join your business and buy your products. What`s wrong with that? But if they don`t, again, these are people you have a connection with anyways.

For The Newest Member

Keep this all so simple. I love to tell my newest person that this business is all about becoming an expert at making friends. When my new person joins we use the friendships they have built to get their first couple of sales. We use it to get referrals and get more content to people. We encourage people to get into groups and grow their network. One of the first things I do is have them learn how to make friends that can last a lifetime and grow your business through connections.

Myself and my team focus on curiosity posts and attraction marketing. You can read more about that in this book. I tell my team that my entire friends list is a warm market. Too many people are missing that connection. You have to build the friendship first. You can become an expert at making friends. You can reach out and make authentic connections with people and not spam them. This business is the people business, go out and meet people!

When you have authentic relationships with people, that builds the trust that I talked about. And, if the time comes that they need the products or opportunity that you offer, they trust you. They aren`t getting products or starting a business from the random person on Facebook. They are coming to a friend. They`re willing to take the leap with you. Build the friends, build the trust, and the business will follow.

Simple Isn't Easy

It doesn't matter at what level you are, this business is hard. Maybe you have been at this awhile and haven't had the success in network marketing that you were expecting. Is that you? You may be scratching your head and thinking, "But she just told me this is simple ." It is! But simple doesn't mean easy. You have to be willing to do consistent work while getting a clear mindset and doing personal development. Some people think that just because they are lower ranks they are the only ones that want to quit. It's not true. I've been a multiple six figure earner for eight years and I still have those moments where I think maybe this industry isn't for me. I know better, but man, some days are tough! This business requires work. I love the work, but let me be clear, it is still work. If I am not always doing my personal development, I have those days that I want to quit. I have to be doing consistent work on my business and mindset.

I always feel like I am trying to keep everyone happy, instead of doing things that are going to make me happy. It's hard because as a woman, I feel like I have to be everything to everyone. I am in a constant state of feeling like I have to balance everything, you know? I have to really work on reminding myself that I am human. I have to keep my vision clear and stop wearing everyone else's expectations around my neck. It isn't easy. And when the weight gets too heavy, I dig into personal development HEAVILY.

I call it Personal Development Immersion Therapy. That is what gets me back into not thinking that I can take care of everyone and please everyone. That is what gets me back to consistency and showing up for my business.

I will listen to audible and podcasts all day. I will cram so much good stuff into my brain that there is no room for the bad. When I start to see that I am allowing it in, I zone in with personal development and get my head straight. This is a process that has to be worked on and a muscle that has to be strengthened. No one has a bulletproof mindset without working on it. Success in this industry doesn`t mean that we don`t have obstacles. Sometimes I feel myself being pulled back and forth as a business woman, wife, mom, and all of the other parts I play. Some days, I am 100 percent for my family, and my team only gets 50 percent of me. Or, it flips flops. Sometimes, I look at other top earners and what they have or have accomplished, and I have to realize that some people have less kids, older kids or a different lifestyle where they can work at a different level in this season of their lives. As a mom with young kids, I am in a different season than some of them. 2020 and this pandemic has led me to a new season even still. I have reached this point where I have found that I have to be willing to give more time to my family. I have to be intentional about it, because I love to work. It is something I have worked on a lot this last year, because I don`t want my team thinking that this is the way to do it. I don`t want my team to see me go go go and give less to myself and my family and think that they have to do that too in order to succeed. It really can burn you out. Setting the right example for my team is so important to me.

I believe we need to run our mindset on the offense. Preventative care if you will. We need to work on personal development BEFORE we are faced with an obstacle. It comes down to plugging into personal development a minimum of 30 minutes a day. It helps me get through those moments when I feel like I am letting things fall between the cracks or when I just don`t feel like I am meeting my potential.

No matter how long you have been in the industry, you have to be a student daily! Always be focused on your own personal growth. Every top earner in this industry will tell you that they spend time daily growing themselves. Working to be better than the person and leader they were yesterday. We are always learning and growing, and we are also leading and innovating at the same time.

What It's All About

Network marketing has made our family a full-time family. I have always dreamed of being a stay-at-home mom. But, what I never dreamed of was being a stay-at-home mom and having my husband be a stay-at-home dad too! We are a full-time family and have been for seven years and counting. Five years ago, we bought our first RV and set a new goal. The goal was to sleep in our RV more than in our home all summer long. And I am so stoked to say we have made that a reality for three years and counting.

Being able to adopt our daughter from China has been possible because of this business. Our daughter was what is known as a "medical expedite" in the adoption world. Which means from the day we saw her face to the day she came home was four months. We had four months to raise enough money to get her home. It was over $40k to bring her home. We were able to do it because of this industry. More than that, since her adoption, we have been able to give away tens of thousands of dollars to other families in the process of adopting. It has not only impacted our family, but we have been able to help so many other families, as well.

The impact for me has been being able to impact other people. Our kids are six, seven, and ten, and we are able to give back to our community as a family. We always are looking at how we can give back and get more babies to homes. The impact has been massive.

There was a time when I was so comfortable with our income, I felt like I had gotten stuck. I called a mentor and asked her how I could say I want more money when we were in a good place. And she said something to me that to this day is what drives me. She said, "Amber, how can you give away millions the way you want to if you aren`t making millions?" Thanks to that conversation, my vision became clear. Make millions so I can give freely and limitlessly. This industry gives me the limitless vision to be able to do that.

This vision? This success? It is for you, too! There is no limit to the potential of this industry. Remember when I was the spammy woman doing the business? I thought I didn`t have too much to lose and so I leapt! I had zero sales experience, hated public speaking, and there I was, working 18 parties a month standing in front of women and selling my face off. I was spamming the world trying to sell, because I was desperate to make sure my family was okay.

When I was a brand new mom, I realized something about the company I was with. I was basically doing a glorified sales job. If I wasn`t working, I wasn`t getting paid. I had taken six weeks off, and without the parties, I had no income. I wanted to find a true network marketing company that would pay me a residual income for the work I was doing.

After selling my husband`s golf clubs to keep our lights on, a friend showed me what true residual income looked like in network marketing, and I was all in. I knew I could sell my face off and I had an even bigger drive because I could sell and have residual. Now that I know what true residual income is, I`d claw through a friggin brick wall to have it. And you should too!

I am sitting in my office right now, and there is a note on my chapter that says "We need a great finish, what do you think?" And, I stared at that question after all of my edits and I thought, how in the heck do I shut this down? What can I even say at this point to you that can make you see your limitless potential? What can I say to you that makes you see your value and your worth? I`m just a stranger to you at this point, right? But, here is what I know. I have read many books like the one you`re holding. And, from each book like this, I have found something that helped me spin something awesome into my business. I read a book like this when I bought my first kit and my husband looked at me and said, "I have your back, but I think you`ve been scammed." And, I was so dang broke. Not just financially, I was just in this place where something had to give. I was meant for more and I just couldn`t figure out what that even looked like. I`d hear about people in this industry making ten thousand dollars a month and I`d think, "Man, good for them. But, that doesn`t happen to people like me." Still, I`d read everything I could. I relied on other people`s belief in me and in this industry. Sometimes, I still rely on that.

But, as I sit here writing a chapter for a book .. by the way, being a published author has been a dream of mine since I was thirteen years old ... I can`t help but look around and think...man, a kit and a dream and a whole lot of obstacles landed me here, closing out a chapter for you. It`s funny because just hours before this moment, I sat down on a zoom with my financial planner. You see, for the last several years, my husband and I have dreamed of buying ten acres in South Carolina and building our dream home. But, to make that dream a reality, we decided we wanted to be debt free except for our mortgage and still have money saved. Sounds reasonable...except that means paying off two new vehicles and our year-old RV. That is the plan. It is a three- plan. It is what we have worked for. It`s what we know needs to happen before we move. Today, our financial planner ran all our numbers and told us that in THIRTEEN MONTHS, we are there! Debt free except our mortgage and ready to buy those then plus acres!

I`m telling you this for a reason. And it isn`t to gloat. It`s because I used to have to charge my groceries and pray my card didn`t decline. And now I have a friggin financial planner.

And listen to me. You may be reading this right now and thinking "woo freaking hooooooo, Amber. But, that stuff doesn't happen for people like me."

You're in luck, friend. That kind of stuff doesn't happen for people like me either ;)

Go all in. Success IS for you. It DOES happen to people like you! People like you who read all the things, implement all the things, make all the friends, and put in the dang work! Before you know it, you'll have THE Rob Sperry in your inbox asking you to write a chapter in his upcoming book too!

Success is for you, and I am lending you my belief in you like so many others have done for me. Put it to good use and make those millions!

> **Coaches Notes:** Amber is the real deal. My favorite part about this whole section is her intertwining her struggles. Success is a process not an event. The sooner you realize this the sooner you can focus on creating your success story. The sooner you realize that the most important recruit is YOU the sooner you can focus on solutions. No, this business won't be easy. All you need to know is that you can have success at this business and that it is 100% worth it. Your struggles are only your story if you make it that way.
>
> Your mess is only your message if you make it that way.
>
> Your tests are only your testimony if you make it that way.

You can make excuses or you can create a success story, but you can't do both. You must first DECIDE that you are going to do whatever it takes to achieve your goals. This commitment will help you get through the emotional rollercoaster that is network marketing.

Author: Monica Fagundes

- Five years of experience in Network Marketing

- Team is currently 5,200 strong, producing twenty seven million dollars in volume in less than three years

- Top twenty team in the company

- Wife and Mother of Five

- Speaker, coach and trainer who is passionate about choosing happiness and branding herself.

"Don't Let a pebble trip you up your mountain"

- Me

Starting your network marketing business can be thrilling and also maybe the scariest thing that you have ever done. I understand. I found network marketing when I hit rock bottom. In my life. In my career. I became a stay-at-home mom because my mental health had taken a severe turn, depression and anxiety were controlling me and I needed to step away and focus on me and my daughter. I have a background in finance and left the industry to work in the non-profit sector which I loved but knew something had to give in my life. I knew that I needed to get out of the toxic relationship I was in at the time, which was contributing to my depression and daily struggles. . I knew I had to do something I had never done before. I needed to choose me. I needed to take a risk for the first time in my life.

If you feel drawn to this industry, I have some advice for you. Just do it. Don`t wait. If it is in your heart and you can`t stop thinking about it; to have more, change other people`s lives, and be your own boss. It is time to leap. I knew that my life needed to change, but that it wouldn`t change with me doing the same thing over and over again. Something had to give.

That pit in the stomach that holds you back is not forever. If something is speaking to you or lights a fire inside of you, it means you are doing the right thing and just keep going. It is going to be hard work and it is going to be soul searching, but it is going to be worth it because you are worth it. You are enough.

I am going to share the strategies that I have used in my own business, and that I use to train my team to help build a successful network marketing business. Even though I am a woman that comes from wall street, it doesn`t take my experience or education to do this business.

Coaches Notes: I sure appreciate Monica being vulnerable, and I hope you do as well. Too many people think that most leaders didn't have massive struggles. Too many people think that either you are instantly great at network marketing or you are not. Doctors and attorneys spend 8 to 12 plus years on schooling to learn their craft. I am in no way saying that it will take that long, but I am saying that everything worthwhile is always harder than we think it is going to be. That is a success principle. Monica had some major struggles that she fought to overcome. She didn't allow her fears to beat her dreams, and she is going to give you the strategy on how she did so.

Face The Fear First

I know the biggest fear I faced when I first started out was the fear of what other people would think. I started an all new Facebook account so that my people who knew me wouldn`t know what I was doing. I only had a few people that I knew following me. Huge tip, don`t do that!

I was terrified of telling people what I was doing. I only added people who I knew online. Looking back now as a six-figure earner for four-plus years, I can`t believe I was allowing the noise to be there.

You have to sit and think about what is holding you back from sharing your life and what you are doing. I personally saw that I was afraid of people judging me – people who I didn`t even really like. They were judging me anyway, so why was I letting their judgments hold me back from creating something? Why did I care?

My grandmother had a saying that kept coming back to me. She told me, "If people are talking about you, they are leaving somebody else alone that isn`t as strong as you." My Nana has passed away, but this is the woman who raised me and was my best friend. I realized that she would never want me to play small or not show up because of what other people were saying about me. But I was letting the noise win. It wasn`t until I met my now husband that I was reminded of this. I finally had someone that believed I could do anything I put my mind to, and he was right! That helped me to start showing up and not hiding behind my fear. You have got to do the same. The strategies that I share don`t work from a place of hiding.

Coaches Notes: As I said in my book The Game of Conquering the mother of all fears is the fear of judgment. Monica is an insanely talented and incredible leader. She still struggled with this basic fear. I struggled so badly with the fear of judgment that I didn`t even make one post on social media for years on anything pertaining to network marketing. This was even after I had made over a million dollars. Monica had to rationalize with herself that everyone will judge you no matter what, so why allow other people`s opinion of you hold you back from chasing your dreams??? As Monica mentioned, no good strategies work from a place of hiding!

Social Strategy

Attraction marketing is the answer and key to the future for all businesses in general. Especially in the times and climate that we live in now. I always go back to the example of Coca Cola and the red can. When you see that specific red what do you think of? I think of cute polar bears, snow, and the commercials of them sledding down during Christmas time. That came from when I was a little girl sitting on my Nana`s shag carpet and watching the tv. It wasn`t about the bears, it was about a company that knew how to attract people to its product. It has now sold billions and even to this day when I see 'that red,` those memories will come flying back and bring joy. . They did attraction marketing the right way, where you can just see a color and think about their product.

People get to know me and they know how much I love a sphynx cat. They see a sphynx cat somewhere else, and my name or picture pops up into their head. I want them to think of me, the person, first. This is how attraction marketing works.

My biggest system is the 80/20 rule. You MUST use your personal account; it is the key to your success. 80 percent of your content should be informative, funny, entertaining, and help people get to know you. Only twenty percent should be about your business or sales. That strategy has been huge for me. I am a huge numbers person, and being able to track and have a system with percentages have been key. I also love the number three. So think about how you are going to use it in attraction marketing. You are going to post three times a day, three different times, and three different types of posts. If you can do that consistently, it will get you where you need to go.

I also find sticking to motto schedules, like terrific Tuesday, or wind down Wednesday can be super helpful. It is easy to get overwhelmed with posting when you start this business. If you can get yourself a motto schedule that will fit your needs, it can help to give you some guidance when you go to post. You shouldn`t be doing "wine Wednesday" if you don`t drink wine! It doesn`t make sense. Put your individual brand into your motto schedule.

It is essential to sit down and write out your social media for the week. If you are a visual person, write it out. If you are able to be a planner, think through your motto schedule and what that will look like. I always do a Motivational Monday and stick to three posts a day minimum. When I am able to map out a week before I do any posting, I can have the photo all ready to go and know what the text is going to be. This saves me time, as well, because I am not wasting time sitting with my social media open just thinking about what to post. I prewrite my script so that when my timer goes off on my phone, I just copy and paste. Don`t allow yourself to make excuses and do find systems and strategies that work for you.

There is a specific impact that attraction marketing has made on my team. I have had two large teams in my Network marketing career. My biggest thing was my struggle with my eating and my weight. I was over three hundred pounds, and I was posting about people embracing and accepting themselves wherever they are at. With that, I have an entire network of women that know me through my journey. I decided to have the sleeve surgery and they have been with me as I have shared that on social media the entire way. I have been candid. A lot of people only put the pretty out there. Attraction marketing is about being authentic, and I have built a tribe of women around that. I have women that have decided to believe in themselves. It has been amazing. I have been open and honest with the struggles that I have gone through and have shown people how authenticity is amazing.

I think it brings people in when we can be honest. I am amazing at business, but I struggle. I have five kids. Three are my biological kids, and two bonus kids. It is a struggle to run a business, have a relationship, and be a mom. I want people to see that it is ok to have a bad day and make that easy mac and cheese instead of a homemade meal. I have shared my struggles with anxiety and depression in a positive way to make it real. You don`t need to continue to grow the stigma about it. That has gotten me so many people contacting me over the years and telling me thank you. People love to follow a story. Your life is a story. Choose to show the real, even when it is a beautiful disaster. You should be doing attraction marketing from day one. Go back and do an inventory of your social media. Go back and look at the last ten posts that you have done. Look and ask yourself, "Do I want to be friends with them? Do I trust this person? Do I like what they post? Do I want to do business with them?" If your posts make you feel negative, or you don`t like what you see, it is time to change. You can do it today.

Your main page is your cover letter. If your cover letter is weak, no one is going to want to read your resume, aka your posts. Make sure your main page is inviting and that it really showcases who you are. Do something simple right now. Go to your profile. If you don`t have a picture of yourself, change it. Make your profile something that people can see and instantly know who you are. People want to see who they are buying from.

Stay Consistent

The social strategy I have shared will only work if you do one thing. Stay consistent. Honestly, the number one thing I did to have success in this business is staying consistent. It is so hard in this life to stay consistent, but I find that it is possible if you really try and take it one step at a time. Give your business the first twenty four hours, then the next step is the first seventy hours to hit certain markers and go from there. It takes three weeks to make a habit and three months to make it a permanent part of your routine. If you can start that first 24 hours and keep building, you can do anything and form that consistency in your business. You must be creative, but you don`t have to reinvent the wheel here. You have to problem-solve things that aren`t working for you, that may be working for other people. It is just a problem that needs to be solved.

I have always loved puzzles. I look for problem solving as a challenge that I embrace and I don`t fear. That has been key in my success in this business. I embrace it, and don`t allow fear to control my life anymore. You have to keep going and consistently keep trying. You can have success.

Be positive. I believe in being authentic and sharing whatever is happening. But there is always a way to spin it in a positive light. You could post and complain about your ex-husband and what he did today or you could spin it a different way like this, "Hey mama sending you lots of love and positive light today. I know my day hasn`t gone the way I wanted it to go but tomorrow will be better."

Companies have literally been demolished by the negative things they have posted or the way they have come across on social media. Don`t be one of those businesses. I know that if I am sitting there plugging my agenda, I am affecting myself, my 5,000 plus team members, and even my other fellow network marketing people in our company. You have a responsibility to kind of be a neutral place.

Look at your content. See what you see. Use engagement posts to get people involved. People love to get involved. If you are doing a remodel in your house ask people which back splash they like best. It is a fun way to have people engage in your posts.

The main thing that holds people back in this industry is what I call listening to the noise. That is people around you in your warm market that are just going to be negative. They are going to tell you that you are silly for doing this or that it is a bad investment. People have such a fear of stigma anyway. Bad companies are everywhere, but people allow other people`s opinions to be the excuse to stop them. If people can quit listening to that, and get out of their own way, they can do anything. Drown out the noise.

This business doesn`t have to be hard. You have to just do the simple things consistently and watch what you can create. Network marketing has been able to make my dreams come true. It has enabled me to reach my high potential. I don`t say full potential, because I am not done yet!

I believe in evolving and always being better and wanting to change, adapt, and evolve. I can have a career where I continue to grow and become a better person. I am now financially stable and not reliant on anyone. I am in charge of my life, and I sleep well at night knowing that I am impacting other people`s lives for the better.

I don`t always choose the easy road, but in response to that is that I get back so much. I get to empower women, and that is everything to me. I get to raise my kids and be there, be present. And when I am in a funk and need to take a couple of hours to myself, I can do that. Because of this business, I get to do it my way. I have learned happiness is a choice, and I am choosing just that.

Coaches Notes: Monica is very deliberate with her social media. She mentioned how she takes time to plan out her social media for the entire week. When used correctly social media is the great amplifier. It increases your warm leads, conversations, and invites about your product or business. Social media done wrong becomes a black hole of time wasting. Be deliberate on social media. Be you. That sounds funny, but so many struggle to show their uniqueness on social media. Be deliberate on posting what your interests and opinions are because your vibe will attract your tribe. If you try to be everything to everyone you will be nothing to no one. Niches to riches. Identify your niches and interests. Then focus on those.

Author: Hillary Hall

- First time network marketer

- Has earned corporate incentive trips

- Team has done over nine million dollars in sales.

- In one day, team did over 190 thousand in sales

- Corporate Regional Trainer

- Lover of lashes and subscription boxes

"Your Excuses are INVALID"

I want to share with you how even the shyest, quietest person can do this business. When you hear that network marketing is an equal opportunity business, it is true! That includes being an equal opportunity for personalities, as well. I have always been a pretty shy and quiet person. I grew up watching my very outgoing mother do network marketing, and I never felt like it was for me, because I wasn`t as outgoing as she was (and still is). When I started I wasn`t great at building relationships, and I couldn`t figure out how I was going to build a business that was all about people. If I struggled talking to people, how in the heck was I going to make this work? I was so shy and timid that I could barely speak my name to people when I was introduced to them. In a group of people, I would really be closed off and wouldn`t be able to look people in the eye.

Coaches Notes: Hillary has had a complete transformation. She identifies as a fellow introvert who has transformed into whatever she wants. I still remember her coming to my Sundance mastermind. This particular mastermind is called the breakthrough mastermind and is specifically geared for those who haven`t yet made six figures in a year. Hillary went on to become the first to attend and graduate to figures and attend the Leader of Leaders mastermind retreat with six to seven figure earners from all different companies. I point this out because she will tell you just a few years ago, she didn`t think this was possible. She felt that her personality was way too timid to have success. Her so-called perceived weakness was a strength but she just didn`t know it, nor did she allow her quietness to be a strength. She pushed herself to get uncomfortable and over time became that conqueror. I couldn`t be more proud and I am excited for you to learn from her in this next section.

Own It For Yourself

This industry is made for everyone, but you have to be willing to work and learn. You have to be willing to change and evolve. It sometimes feels uncomfortable or painful, but it is your ability to do it anyways that matters.

When I first joined, I was still shy, but my desire to succeed was so much bigger than my excuses. I was in a low income situation, and I was desperate to get my kids and myself out of there. I needed to not be living in there and not be living off of food stamps and government assistance.

To me, going to school full time to become a phlebotomy technician was my ticket out. I was a single mom at the time living in low income housing and feeding my kids with food stamps. After months of watching my mom with her company I decided to give Network Marketing a go because of the success she has been having.

I had absolutely no personal background doing network marketing before starting the company that I am in now. Growing up watching my mom do it and doing it myself were completely different! Even though I had watched my mom for thirty years do different network marketing companies, it was still such a challenge for me to translate her business into the vision for my own future.

She wanted me to join back when she started this company, and I just couldn`t see it, Network Marketing just wasn`t my thing. I wanted to stick with school and get a job to pay my bills. That was what I thought my path was for life. I watched as my mom did well the first and second months in this business, and then she exploded her third month. I was always her biggest cheerleader.

She encouraged me again and told me she thought I should do this, so I finally gave in. I thought I really couldn`t lose anything by trying. My thought was, "If it pans out, it pans out." And it did.

 I always watched my mom get to a certain point and she would stop. She never really hit it big before the company we are in right now, and I think a huge part of that was her belief in herself. It is when she found Rob Sperry and this company that her business took off. I had to take the belief in her and her success and own that I wanted to have my OWN success. I couldn`t just piggyback my success to hers. This is huge for starting a business. You can get excited and motivated about other people and what they are doing, but you can`t think that their success or vision is going to translate to you. You must be willing to have your own vision. You have to create your own why, and you have to start getting your own success.

As soon as I had my own vision, drive, and why, my business started to be strong, just like my mom had with this company. I hit every goal and rank and I did it quickly. It was amazing to me to see that when I used a system coupled with belief and ownership, I could have this business work for me. I was so grateful that I hadn`t let my thoughts hold me back from joining and doing network marketing for myself. I am so grateful that I didn`t play the timid card and just piggyback on my mom`s success. I am so proud of myself for creating the vision, drive, and success that I have.

> **Coaches Notes:** This part really stood out to me. "This industry is made for everyone, but you have to be willing to work and learn. You have to be willing to change and evolve. It sometimes feels uncomfortable or painful, but it is your ability to do it anyway that matters." There is an essay called The Most Common Denominator of Success where the author spent a good deal of his life studying the difference between those who are successful

vs those who aren`t. Listen to what the Author Albert Gray said. "The common denominator of success — the secret of success of every man who has ever been successful — lies in the fact that he formed the habit of doing things that failures don`t like to do." It isn`t like the successful love being judged and rejected. It is that they are WILLING to do what they need to because their purpose is bigger than the fears.

Watch And Learn

I watched my mom while growing up as she tried over and over again with companies in network marketing. She would have parties, talk to everyone about what she was doing, and really network and get to know people.

When I was sixteen, my mom got sick and couldn't go and do one of her home parties. I had watched and listened to her give the presentation so many times that she asked me to go and do it for her. Even though I was terrified, I filled in for her that night. I sold $1k and booked five parties from that all on my own. How did I do that? I had watched and learned how she did it and I just modeled what she did.

That is all we do in network marketing! Get good at watching your mentor and listening to the words they say. Our industry is built on people that are good at watching, learning, and duplicating. Maybe talking to people isn't your thing. Maybe you feel like you don't know what to say. That's ok! It is something that can be learned. You can learn today what to say tomorrow.

My mom has played a pivotal role in helping me learn how to connect with people. She has always been a social butterfly, but I just didn't see it as being beneficial when I was growing up. When I got into network marketing I saw why that skill was so important. It wasn't this crazy tactic, she just taught me how to ask questions, and be interested in others. It is that simple.

Network marketing isn't a nine to five gig. You can't be that closed off person that doesn't talk to anyone.

Here is the good thing though; you don`t need to have the relationship skills right now. You can learn them! Anyone can learn how to build relationships. Just like I learned. This isn`t just going to come to you. You have to put yourself out there and see what clicks with people. You have to see what people connect with you about. Use the systems in this book and stick with them. They will teach you how to start to interact in person and online. I always say, see what you are not good at, and then go out and learn how to do that. Everything can be learned.

Facebook System

One of the key areas that I learned to build relationships in on Facebook. This is also a place that I didn't really interact that much. I had social media to connect with friends to see what they were up to and see their pictures, but I wasn't engaging and being part of anything.

Building relationships is so important. You must be on Facebook or social media building consistent relationships. When I say consistent relationships, I mean interacting with people on a regular basis. You can't just add someone as a friend, write one comment on one post and then move on. You have got to be there for people. You have to engage with them and be there for them if they need support. I learned really quickly in the beginning that if I didn't have relationships and people, I wouldn't have a community. You can't grow if you don't build relationships with people.

As you are building those consistent relationships, you must be building them authentically. I always tell my team that they can't be sending out a thousand messages and joining a thousand groups. Because if you do that, there is no way you can stay consistent and authentic with the connections you are making.

Here is a great strategy to help with Facebook. When you first start go out on Facebook, find 3 groups to join. They have to be groups that you are actually interested in. So go find the hiking group, the pug group, or the mom of a toddler group. Join to engage with the community and people. Get to know them and start commenting, liking, and posting things that have to do with the group topic. You don't have to be or should you be pushing your product. You have to be real and start being part of the group. Be yourself and be consistent.

As you engage with people more, they will start looking at your profile and seeing what you are doing. This is a great time to start sharing with people what you do. The very newest network marketers are usually so afraid of the stigma that goes with network marketing. You must be able to get over that because this is a legitimate business. This will feed your family and can get you in a better spot. This is also an opportunity to bless other people with a product or an opportunity.

A lot of times I will spend time interacting with people on their post and looking to see where I can help. I have been there before. I have needed other people to help me and it always meant so much to me when people helped me. If I see a post where someone is in need, I will reach out to them in messenger and let them know about the opportunity that I have for them. It is all personalized to them and our relationships.

Think about what you are posting and how it is being seen by other people. You can`t just put up a graphic of your company or product and think that people are going to come to you and buy. It just doesn`t work that way. There are so many great tips in this book about how to craft your post and make it engaging. Use them. Work on your craft of posting. Just like I said before, learn how to do it!

Another tip to help you get better engagement is to go live every day or every other day. This is a way for more people to see what you are doing. You can go "live" about your product or something completely different. Whatever it is you have to build those relationships with people. My last tip for social media is use the network you have. I love to be able to reach out to people that I have been friends or am currently friends with that I am not friends with on Facebook. You have people in your life right now that you are associated with, but you aren`t connected on social media. Get connected!

Social media is a great way to reconnect and have people that you already know start to see what you have been up to. I will also send them a message and tell them "thanks for the add" It helps Facebook see that we have more of a connection than just a random friend add.

As a shy person, I went from having 100 friends to having 1300 friends on Facebook over the past couple of years. This was all because of my willingness to learn and put myself out there. Sometimes doing things like going "live" can be scary. You have to be willing to do it anyways. I promise you it will be worth it, and here is a hint: It gets easier every time you do it. Now I can do a live and not even think twice about it!

The Drive To Succeed

As soon as I set out with my own goals, I had a drive and determination to get to my next goal accomplished. It helped me stay consistent with social media. I had a life that I was ready to get out of, but it wasn`t just going to happen for me.

I had to go all in with network marketing, because it was my only option. I had to run for the next level of our compensation plan, and I had to make sure that I kept pushing. I kept my eye on the next rank always. I remember when I was still living in low income housing and working hard to make this work. We hit the next rank, and I realized that this was it. I could finally do what I had set out to do for me and my kids. I started looking for a house and it was the best feeling ever to know that I could do that. We ended up finally moving out of low income housing, a year after signing up, getting off of food stamps knowing that I was the one that made that possible.

A year after that, we bought a house!! The best day ever, but I wasn`t going to stop there. That was just my first step. After that, it felt like a weight was lifted from me, and I was ready to see what else I could accomplish.

Every time I hit a goal in the beginning it felt like that financial goal was lifted a bit more. It helped me be consistent. I had a goal to do this, and when I saw that it was actually possible, it just made me drive that much harder.

I wanted to share this because I think sometimes people don`t see what is possible for them. They think that getting themselves out of low income housing isn`t something they could do. I think one of my strengths is seeing people`s potential before they can see it themselves.

I love being able to open people up to what is possible for their lives. Because I believe that everyone has the possibility to do this and make it work.

Recently, I had a new recruit that couldn`t see what was possible. She would get down on herself, and just see herself as a failure. I remember being there, and I just talked to her like I would have wanted to be talked to when I was in that spot. She just told me that she has made one thousand dollars this month. How amazing is that? She did that. She was the one that set out on the goal path and even when it got hard, she kept showing up. She needed me to remind her of what she could do, but it was all her that did it.

Sometimes just casting that vision and letting people know that you are on their side is awesome. When you cast a vision for people you have to remember why they decided to join, and then you have to remind them. Listen and see what they are wanting, and then cast the vision. Maybe they need to pay rent, or maybe put gifts under the tree. You have to know what they want and then cast the vision.

When people ask me what network marketing has done for me, I always answer, "What has it not done for me?" Honestly, it has helped me grow my confidence, leadership skills, time and money freedom. The list can go on. But I think the number one thing that network marketing has taught me is that anything can be learned if you are willing to be the student. I want to encourage you to be willing to invest in your learning. Be willing to be the student of this industry and learn how this can work for anyone. Go after those goals and surround yourself with people that believe in you, even if you can`t believe in yourself. Your life is as bright as you want it to be.

Coaches Notes: There is a huge lesson to learn from Hillary. She says that she had to go all in because it was her only option. If you treat this business casually, it will become a casualty. Too many people treat this business like a hobby and then wonder why it never worked. Look, I get it. Most of you reading this book are busy. We are all busy. The key is when you work to actually focus on the income producing activities and FOCUS!

Author: Holly Highfield

- Achieved top ranks in her company in less than three years

- With the help of her team, she has generated more than 36 million in sales across 20 countries and counting.

- Proud toddler-boy momma

- Loving and supportive wife

- Certified Youth Nutritionist

- Never met a fur-baby she didn`t like

- 20 years in corporate world - banking

"There are no limits to what you can accomplish except the limits you place on your own thinking."

- Brian Tracy

How would you like to become a fearless recruiting machine? If you answered yes, you are reading the right book.

The coach in me wants to help people win and succeed in the goals they set for themselves. This chapter is all about helping you see your potential in this industry. There are four keys you must have to successfully recruit without fear. I promise you that if you can follow these keys, you will become a fearless recruiting machine that can create the type of freedom that our family has been able to create with network marketing.

Having the right mindset is vital to success with anything you do. Whether it is, weight loss, improving your relationships, or building a business. Skills and systems can be taught, but if you don't have the right mindset in place, you will find it hard to stick to any system and stay consistent.

A recruiter's mindset can be challenging. But it is attainable. When I started, I came to the table with limiting beliefs. I am a recovering people pleaser. I let other people's opinions dictate how I showed up and who I shared the opportunity with. Can you relate to this? These four key strategies kept me on the right track to success. They can do the same for you, but you must follow the system. The keys only work if you work the keys.

> **Coaches Notes:** Pay attention. I have had the great privilege of personally coaching Holly. I will tell you that she is a leader that leads by example. She is willing to do whatever it takes. She is impressively diligent and organized. She is going to give you some tough love on how you can achieve the recruiter's mindset, which is where it all begins. The breakdown in this section is one you will want to not only read but you will want to study. This section will give you the blueprint for creating a bulletproof mindset.

Key #1 –BELIEVE IN YOU: Believe that YOU ARE a person worthy of abundance. YOU ARE valuable and worth partnering with. TRUTH - you won`t get paid until someone joins; however, you have to believe that you are worth locking arms with. You must be that person you want to enroll. *Like often attracts like.* If you don`t have a belief in yourself, people that you talk to will sense it.

Example: The dreaded chicken list...Be honest, do you have at least ONE PERSON you KNOW and still have not reached out to? GUILTY! Many of us do or did. I know I had many of them when I was getting started. Why... fear of...

> *Judgment for my LACK OF SUCCESS*
> *Judgment for my LACK OF KNOWLEDGE*
> *Judgment because IT'S NETWORK MARKETING*

When these thoughts creep in....*STOP!!* Rip off the band-aid and just ASK! Everyone starts somewhere. Not to mention, you`re learning from the *BEST of the BEST* in this industry! You invested in this very book loaded with amazing ideas, strategies and stories from more than a dozen people. This tells me you really want this. Consider all your mentors. You can then teach them the way! If you don`t have the belief now, STEAL it from someone else! You MUST get rid of the negative talk. Because if you don`t believe in you, those you approach won`t either. YOU ARE WORTHY!

If this is an area where you fall short, feed your brain with positivity and belief of what you are capable of. Write positive affirmations on your bathroom mirror or sticky notes where you can see them. "You will impact someone today." "You are meant for great things." "You are the architect of your life." "I am and will always be enough." "I am focused on my goals and feel passionate about my work." "I will live my full potential." Post them anywhere and everywhere you look. Say them out loud. Put them in a gratitude journal at night. Do this until you believe it.

After 20 years of banking, I didn't know much else. My life was my job. Despite my success in my work, it was very difficult for me to believe enough in myself to do something different. Throughout my career, I always had others guiding or directing me to the next new role or position. I worked my way up. Can you relate? It was that experience that reminded me that the new role was just that. I had to learn each new position by doing, shadowing those who were already doing it, and be coachable. Willing to implement what I was learning to improve, just a little each day. It was this thought process and approach that got me on the track to believe in myself for my network marketing business. This leads us to the next key.

Key #2 – BELIEF IN WHAT YOU HAVE: Believe 100 percent in what you have to offer - your company, products, services and opportunity. If your belief wavers, then those you are talking to will sense that and it will feel more like "selling" than providing a service.

Believe what you are offering is more than just a product or service. It's a GIFT. Something of HIGH VALUE. Treat it like gold. It's our job to help them see the value and want it for themselves. Don't be afraid to take it away! Yep, I said it. I do the take-away often. POSTURE is key!

Nothing someone says or does should make you question what you are offering. It will be tough. Those you care the most about will challenge you. Even if your closest friend or family member says, "It's a scam!" And let's be honest, those closest to us can be the WORST! I know! Even after the success we've had, I still have my skeptics and haters but here's the TRUTH! Their opinion is just that. It's a reflection of who they are, NOT YOU! Do NOT let the DREAM STEALERS rob you of having the life you desire and deserve.

Key #3 –IT'S NOT UP TO YOU: Our role is to SHARE what we have with EVERYONE. It`s not up to you or me to decide who will or won`t join. I can`t pre-judge who I "think" would be interested let alone good at what I`m doing. It`s not up to me to make decisions for other people. Have you ever found yourself saying "Oh, they wouldn`t be interested because;

- They are way too busy...

- They have plenty of money....

- They are healthy folks...

- They have a lot going on right now...

- They couldn`t afford it...

Think of it this way; If you went out to eat and the waiter didn`t ask what you wanted and just brought you out whatever she wanted to serve you, that would probably rub you the wrong way, right? EXACTLY! NO ONE likes to have people make decisions for them. People want the freedom to decide for themselves. So WHY would you take the opportunity away from them?

TRUTH – you don`t know who is lying awake at night praying for something. Never assume that what you see on the outside is the reality.

I repeat, my role is to share the product and opportunity with everyone. I cannot, should not, and will not prejudge who I think would do good at this or who needs this. You never know who will be successful at this business. As much as you think you know what is going on in someone`s life, you don`t. You don`t know what is keeping them up at night... their hopes... dreams for the future. You just don`t know. Everyone is worthy of hearing about what you have.

Key #4 – DETACH YOURSELF: *"Trade your expectations for appreciation and the world changes instantly."* - Tony Robbins

When meeting and talking with someone, it`s important to go into the conversation unattached. What I mean is, you`ve got to detach yourself from the outcome. If they say yes, no or not now, it doesn`t matter. I get it, easier said than done, but here is why. You`ve got to *manage your EXPECTATIONS.* If you walk into a conversation already envisioning them saying YES, where you`ll place them on your team and what rank you`ll be, you`ll be....

- Setting yourself up for an emotional roller coaster

- Putting pressure on them and yourself

- Come off as salezie, needy or desperate

- Making it uncomfortable to see each other in the future.

If you have preconceived expectations you may be setting yourself up for disappointment. I know because I`ve done it. I used to be so focused on the outcome and what it would mean for me that when they would say no, it was a huge blow to my ego and my drive. Sometimes so much so that I stopped working my business for a day or two. When it shook my belief really bad, I stopped working for a week or longer. Yikes! You can`t get that time back. So, don`t do what I did and waste it. Please learn from our mistakes and failures so you don`t have to.

When you have a recruiter`s mindset, you are focused on being a solution provider. You are focused on what`s in it for them, not you. When you want what`s best for them, you will be more successful.

So, there you have it, my four key strategies to mastering the recruiter`s mindset so you can be a fearless recruiting machine! Let`s recap the four key concepts discussed;

#1 – Believe in yourself

#2 – Believe in what you have

#3 – It`s not up to you

#4 – Detach yourself

Here is your first "call to action." Rate yourself on a scale of 1 – 5 for each of the Key concepts discussed. One being the lowest meaning not very strong at it and five being the highest, the most confident in. "Decide" today what actions YOU WILL take to improve the score in the areas you are not yet a five. Why should you do this exercise?

Improving the score will boost your CONFIDENCE.

Improving the score will Improve your POSTURE

Improving the score will strengthen your BELIEF

Most importantly, it will allow you to successfully recruit more people into your business without fear, to create the life you *DESIRE and DESERVE – ALL while MAKING AN IMPACT.*

My husband and I run a volleyball club which we love! After we help people learn the basics, we build on those basics and make them unstoppable. Once you have learned and are using the keys I have talked about above, I want you to build on them and create an unstoppable business.

Coaches Notes: I want to reiterate one part from Holly`s section. "Believe what you are offering is more than just a product or service. It`s a GIFT. Something of HIGH VALUE. Treat it like gold. It`s our job to help them see the value and want it for themselves. Don`t be afraid to take it away! Yep, I said it. I do the take away often. POSTURE is KEY!" This is the next level recruiting mindset. The business behind the business is always bigger than just the products or opportunity. As Holly said it is a gift. Think about all of the intangible value your company and team provide. It is much bigger than your products or opportunity. Your goal is to start to open up your mind to that and discover how to convey that vision to others. It won`t happen overnight but as you open up your mind, you will become more aware and you will improve your vision/communication skills which will help you up your recruiting game big time.

Now that you know the four keys, time for your POWER PLAYS. These are the concepts and tools that you can use to BUILD on the keys above.

Power Play #1 Learn To Be Coachable. Think about when you started your first day at a new job. You didn`t know much. You had to shadow others. Be coachable. Learn how they wanted you to accomplish tasks. Over time you got really good, if not great, at knowing how to do that job. In network marketing, you join thinking you know some things. You think you have knowledge, experience and know-how.

One of the things we did wrong, in the beginning, is that we didn`t open up the blueprint. We didn`t open up the system and see what others had already mapped out for us. We had success in our jobs and business, so we figured we knew everything we needed to know to be

131

successful in network marketing, too. Mind you, we had never done network marketing. We became so frustrated at not being where we wanted to be in our business that we finally asked, "What are we doing wrong?" When we made the decision to be coachable, to listen to those who were where we wanted to be, and tell ourselves we didn`t know everything, that`s when our business shifted. It allowed us to start to see success.

Power Play #2- Make People Feel Empowered, Confident, and Capable. This one is so powerful but can be a tough one. It goes back to having people skills. You can learn this. You learn to connect and realize that not everyone believes in themselves or thinks they are worthy. You want to support your team members just enough that they see the possibility and know that you are there, while they learn themselves and do it for themselves. This one was difficult for me, being the recovering people pleaser. I never wanted anyone to think I didn`t care. That I wasn`t willing to help or support or answer their questions. However, what I learned was that I was only doing them a disservice.

For example, I have team members call to ask a question. Folks who have been around for a while, are on the calls, join the training etc. Questions that I`m pretty confident they know or know where to go to get the answer. Before, the old me would just give the answer. Now I will say, "Great questions, what do you think?" or "How were you thinking of responding?" Now they are learning to answer their own questions. It helps them feel empowered and I am encouraging them to believe in what they know more and be less reliant on me. This way they can feel capable. Be more confident in what they do know. Plus, as your team grows, you are teaching them to teach their team to be more self-sufficient, empowered and capable.

Power Play #3 What You Lack In Skills You Play In Numbers.

This is a numbers game. Until you get good and master the skills, which you will do, you have got to take action and get the numbers behind them. Some call it "on the job training." You get good at mastering by doing it over and over again. Not by reading book after book or watching endless hours of training videos.

Play the numbers until the skills get there. The more people you talk to the more you make money. A bad invite is better than no invite at all. I repeat, a bad invite is better than no invite. It goes for any skills we are doing. At the end of the day, it is about taking the action.

Early on in my college career I was working doing telemarketing. I sold credit cards. I wasn`t old enough to have one, but I sold them. I knew that I had to get so many sales an hour to hit bonuses and incentives. I knew I had to go through so many no`s. If I stopped focusing on the sales and focused on how many no`s I was getting, I would eventually get the yes. I started tracking the no and yes. It was more no`s. It got me to redirect to the no`s and the yes just started to come. It helped me work on conversations and connecting with people. It was extremely helpful. Play the numbers.

After nearly a decade in this industry, I can see how far I`ve come. However, I also know how much further I have to go. Perhaps you are feeling stuck. Perhaps you were hoping I`d give you the secret to enrolling 10 people a day or a month into your biz. Well... the truth is that your mindset will determine how you show up in your business, if you are going to take the actions necessary to actually make "this thing" work for you. Will you have the discipline to be intentional and block out time on your schedule to work your calendar? Will you set a timer to remind you when to start following up and prospect? Will you be willing to choose a company event over a family birthday party? What trade-offs are you willing to make to achieve the level of success you desire. When I was introduced to this, I was working 50 to 60 hours a week at my job plus helping at the volleyball club on the nights and weekends. I was traveling for tournaments and balancing the needs of friends and family, etc. I didn`t have "time" for another project. Here is the Truth. There will never be the "perfect" time. Life happens to us all. It`s happening to you right now. When I said yes to network marketing, I didn`t know I was going to be let go from my job after 20 years of service. I didn`t know that a year after that, my husband was going to be let go after 23 years from his job. I didn`t know my son would bless us two months early leaving us stranded thousands of miles away from our home, family and friends, living between the NICU and the hotel. Who knew we would be faced with a pandemic that would force us to shut down our volleyball club for a while? It was because we made a "decision." A decision to treat our business as business, not a hobby. A decision that our company events were non-negotiable. We were going to put into "action" what we learned.

I believe there is no such thing as the perfect time to start a business - To PLAY BIG in your business. Life will and always will be happening. How you decide to show up will determine your level of success. As you read this book and learn how others have gotten where they are, just know this. If you:

Believe in yourself and what you have, unapologetically

It`s not up to you to decide who will or won`t

Detach yourself from the outcome to manage your expectations

Learn to be coachable

Make people feel empowered, confident, and capable

And when all else fails, play the numbers

You WILL have the confidence, desire, passion and drive to take the ACTIONS you need to build a long-term, sustainable and lucrative business allowing you to live the life you not only dream of but deserve. All while helping countless others do the same.

Coaches Notes: Holly gets it. Let me summarize what I read and understand. Be the bold version of YOU and always stay coachable. Holly is always reinvesting back into herself. She is always challenging herself to be bolder and to increase her own belief system. Holly is always striving to be better. It is so impressive to watch Holly and her husband continue to strive for greatness. Your goal is progress. Stop making the plan for the plan. Start taking action and believing in yourself.

Author: Holly Lo

- Certified labour doula and childbirth educator
- Canadian Founder of company
- Wife to an amazing man and mama of three miracles
- Highest rank in her company

"I've learned that people will forget what you said, people will forget what you did, but people will never forget how you made them feel"

-Maya Angelou

The most reluctant skeptical customer can become your best builder. I know, because I was that person in the beginning. I was one of those people who refused to do network marketing, but you do crazy things when you are desperate with a sick child. From the time our second child was born to when she was two years old, we were in and out of the hospital with health problems that she was experiencing. It was one of the most helpless times in our lives.

One of my best friends, who I thought would be the last person on earth to try anything natural, showed up with a product from a network marketing company, and I thought she was joking. I was at the end of my rope, and at that point I was willing to try anything. So we tried this product, and our child experienced instant results.

That started me on a journey in network marketing. I had faith and trust in my dear friend, but still aired on the side of skepticism with the industry. I wanted to help my friend out, and was happy to continue to explore the product and buy a kit. But I was not open to doing the business. You may find your best recruit in your customers. That is why nurturing customers and continuing to grow relationships with them is so important.

At this time I owned a baby retail store, I was a doula, and I was a coach. I was basically covering all of these areas for women in the pregnancy and birth phase of life. I told my friend I would sell her product at the shop but still wasn't open to doing the business myself or recommending it to my clients.

So, for four months our family used the product. Step by step day after day I was watching our family's health change, and I couldn't believe that this was all happening because of the network marketing product. Of course, when something like that happens, and you see others struggling, you just start sharing. You may be in the same place

I was at. Maybe you have a product that you have just fallen in love with and you are willing to share, but hesitant to do the business. Ask yourself, what is holding you back?

I know for me it was the skepticism and the pure doubt around the business model. My husband is a brilliant and successful businessman, and he was looking at the business model that the company had. He said, "You are already doing half the business by sharing. May as well talk to your friend and see what the next step is."

It took my husband`s business savvy and my friend`s guidance for me to finally say yes to doing this as a business. As you start recruiting, you may need to think about not only the person in front of you but also think, "Who do they need to support this person as they make this decision?"

My paychecks started growing as I shared, and they got even bigger when I started to take the business seriously. I was amazed but still reluctant to call myself a network marketer or really go all in. It was six months before I really let it sink in that this was real. When I really started to take ownership of the business, I realized I could use my experience in my previous jobs to really make this work. Never give up on your newest recruit. They are coming in with all of these preconceived thoughts about this business. They may be battling with other people`s opinions about what they are doing. It doesn`t mean that they won`t be successful, it just means that they may need more support and guidance just like my friend gave me.

Expos And Events

In my previous job of owning the baby store, I also held a very well-known baby expo in our area each year. When I started network marketing, I knew I wanted to use the expo and event space to promote my business. It was interesting to go from being in charge of the expo to being one of the vendors at the expo. One of the biggest things I learned is that you are not there just to sell stuff. If you can realize that from the start, you will set your expectations up to be more in line with the actual purpose of expos. As the person who has coordinated many expos, I have seen the success and failure at these shows, and there is a definite system for success that I want to share with you.

First, there are some basic things that you must know-

1-Know your event. Know who will be at this event. Know your audience. This is the first key to creating a successful event. I am not going to go to wedding shows. These aren`t my people. My product could sell there, but my target audience is mamas with kids and babies.

2-Know your cost. How much do you have to sell in order to make this event worth it? Know what it is going to cost for you to break even. How do you think you will make your investment back? Is it selling the product? Is it getting one new contact sign up? Know and set your goals.

3-Know how you are going to collect contact information. Have a quick and efficient way to collect contacts. Events are all about the contact information. It is the follow up that is key at these shows. You should be making quick connections and then collecting ways to follow up.

> **Coaches Notes:** There is no one way to build the business. Too many leaders confuse principles with techniques. They teach one way to do the business, and if you don`t do it that way, they end up chastising you. I have had the great opportunity to personally coach Holly. She is one of the most consistent leaders that I know. I love that she is mentioning expos and events because the main principle is to talk to brand new people as that is the #1 income producing activity. Make sure you are planning out your income producing activities like events. You can use The Network Marketing Strategy planner/ tracker that was specifically made for network marketers to plan out events, income producing activities, and your daily methods of operations. Very few talk about expos and events, so this gives you another perspective on how there are so many different ways to have success as long as you follow the key principles.

Success Plans= Successful Events

Know your plan before you go in. See yourself as the brand that is selling a product or opportunity. People won`t remember you if you are just that woman who was selling a product, and they will just go and find someone online with the exact same product when they get home. Brand yourself as the thing they remember. Be the brand that people want to buy the product from.

If you are just the woman at the Christmas market selling the same thing year after year, people aren`t thinking about you as a brand. Another woman could be there the next year, and they wouldn`t know any differently. Be the brand that people remember. It takes time, but if you put a great display, and connect genuinely with people, they will remember you. They will come and look for you, not just the product. Present yourself as the expert in your field and carry yourself this way. Connect with people as your own brand. It does work. At the end of the day, people are buying you.

I always have a goal before I start the event. I have a staff now that helps with events, and it is key that we all have a very defined goal in mind that we are all working towards achieving. Know how many contacts you want to make. Have a focus and be clear on your goal. It helps you to not get sidetracked. And let me be clear, it is easy to get sidetracked at these events! Be laser-focused on the goal. Know how much you have to make to pay for your booth and supplies. How much product or sign-ups do you need? If you go in with no plan, you get nowhere. This goes even for networking events. Know your focus and who you are looking for.

Part of the plan is knowing your target audience and knowing who you are looking for before you go to the event. When you find your target audience, don`t be afraid to reach out and say, "I think I have something for you." Or have something that brings them in. We all get sample overload at events, right? So that is when you find something to draw them in. Know that target audience.

Saying hi is great but that just means you are a nice person. When I spend my time looking for my target audience, I cannot be focusing on saying hi and chatting with everyone, I need to use my time and energy to really bring the right people in. Know who you are looking for and have something for them.

Have something that you have to specifically tell them about. It helps to be able to keep them engaged with you for longer. I say something like, "Can I show you really quickly how to use that?" No one has ever said no.

The Hidden Gems

There is a HUGE hidden gem that most people miss when doing an expo. Some of your best leads will be the vendors that are there selling.

Vendor goody bags have been wildly successful for my team. We always put together fun bags for the vendors. When I was putting on events, I would do this for every single vendor, and I just kept it up. I like to put mini water bottles, a small snack, and add a bit of our products with my card. Vendors are blown away by the fact that we thought about them, and they are intrigued by the product I added.

Don`t be in a rush to leave when the event is over. You miss opportunities to connect with other vendors. I love to connect with vendors because you already know you have something in common. They are business people who are willing to sacrifice their time to make money. They are willing to talk to strangers and engage. It is amazing that you are surrounded by a group of people that you already know are business-minded and willing to do work, yet most just see them as competition. They could be the best contact you get from that event.

Coaches Notes: I love specific strategies you can implement today. Holly gives you the playbook. She gives you the step by step guide. She also gives you the vision that it is a process. Like every process, it is something that will take time and take constant reassessment. Too many network marketers try something and then quickly decide if they are good at that something or not. Success isn`t an event. Success is a process. If you commit to events and expos, you now have the process to focus on so that you can have success.

The Secret Weapon

Events or expos are always going to include a lot of educating. One of your main objectives is to think about how you can teach someone something about your product or business in sixty seconds or less. Quick connections are the name of the game at events. The quicker and catchier, the better.

When my team is going to something like a Christmas fair, I tell them to not go all-in on making a quick connection. You are getting paid on the connection you have. Have you ever gone to an expo and had the person at the booth not even look at you? It is odd and it makes people actually not want to see what you have in your booth. Your whole point is to connect with people.

If you can get a quick connection, great! Now you have to do something with it. You can get your booth paid for with sales, but the ultimate success of a booth is to get their contact information. There are several ways to gather contact info, such as having a drawing, doing a sign-out sample, or just physically asking people if they want to use the product right then.

Let me be clear about another component; booth space is important! Your booth space is your first impression at events and expos. A sad-looking booth makes it seem like you have a sad business opportunity. Too much can overwhelm people and make them steer clear. Keep it clean and simple.

What is your market and what do they need? Make it easy to pick it up, see, taste, touch, smell. Come up with another draw into the booth.

It doesn't always have to be about the product. Not everyone may want it but make the booth interesting for the expo.

We are usually at baby shows because that is my target audience, and I love involving my kids. This is a family business! Our booth is set up to look like a house, and our kids walk around inside the booth or just outside and hand out samples. Who says no to a cute kid asking if they want a sample?! As they do, I have taught them to tell the person, "come and talk to my mom and she will show you what to do with the product." It works. I can't tell you how many people come through because of this technique. Leverage what you have!

One fun thing we did was our kids were doing triathlons all over the place. It was a ton of fun and we wanted to be involved, so we sponsored the event and traveled around with our tent. Our back panel of the tent had permanent markers and anyone that came by that was already using the product, we asked them to come and write what they loved about the product or company.

These people weren't even on our team. They were just customers from different teams telling us what they loved about the company or product. It was brilliant because it gave us a very filled back wall of testimonials. So cool. It was so much fun. People took pictures of it and posted it all over social media. We do it at all of our events now.

You Are Lit

I had an event and invited women to come and learn and try the product. We had a big group come, and I invited my shyest new business builder to the event. I told her that she would be the expert at the table and that she would be the finisher at the end. I gave her the rundown and she had confidence in what she was doing. By the end of the night, she had made friends, connected with people on social media, and closed a couple of things.

I can push and hold your hand at the same time. This just goes right along with being a mom. Sometimes we have to push people. You can`t learn this on paper. You need to be pushed and have the experience. I teach my leaders how to do this as well. I did it with them, and now they do it with their people.

The biggest thing I struggled with at becoming a leader was....being a leader. I remember when my upline told me I was going to do my own team call. I will never forget the feeling inside. I got so angry. I am a very even keel person and I just remember the anger and telling her "NO! NO!" She told me I had a team to lead and they needed to see me. She didn`t accept my no. I felt so put off, because I thought she never told me this was part of the deal. I came on to sell products, not be a leader.

You are a business partner, but I also want you to know, you are LIT. You are a "Leader In Training." At some point, you will be running and leading a team. Most people don`t feel qualified to do this. It is normal, you will be fine. Start right now as seeing yourself as LIT. You will have a moment of stepping up and owning the role of leader. You will have to intentionally grow, and that comes with growing pains at times. But, I see some people fall flat here in leadership. You need to choose to lead and not just be a salesperson. Leadership is on you.

I hope you can use these tips to create a successful network marketing business that can bless your lives and your future team's lives. Before this network marketing journey, our family was in rough shape. Our marriage was almost over, my business was collapsing. We were not in a good place. My motivation may have come from a dark place, but it made the difference. I wanted to show my husband that I could be successful. He helped so much with his connections. He was a successful realtor making great money, but he was never home. The fact that we could do this business, make great money, AND be able to see each other was huge. Now, he has retired from real estate, and we are able to work together while also being able to let each other stay in our own lanes with our abilities. I am forever grateful for the opportunity I had to go from a skeptical customer to a full-blown successful network marketing expert.

Coaches Notes: Every single leader failed their way forward. Every single leader was pushed outside of their comfort zone. Holly specifically mentions how uncomfortable it was. This business is all about leadership which may scare many of you at first. Don't be scared. You have so much support from this incredible profession. Regardless of which company you are in, you are reading this book now and getting support for your business. There are so many paid courses and free content online to help you build your dreams. Just know that your fears are normal. Just know that you aren't alone. Just know that someone has had much less than you and made it happen. You can make this happen! It won't be easy but I promise you that it is worth it.

Author: Boris Lupsina And Marina Mursic

Our life motto is CVMD: creating value and making a difference. If you are not creating value for others you are wasting your time. We all can make a difference in this world. Everyone should remember that when you receive, your hands are full. But when you give, your heart is full. So, let`s make a difference together!

Working as a couple which has led to a deeper, stronger connection between us

- Built a team of almost 80,000 team members in just five years, in more than 20 countries and four continents

- Became one of the best paid young couples in network marketing

- Moved to our dream house on the island (Canaries)

- Became parents to a beautiful little baby girl Sky Lylah *(We don't have words to describe the hope this baby gives us for the future. A new reason to do even more and better in the future)*

CONGRATULATIONS! Your journey to financial freedom has begun! It is our honor to be able to share with you a bit about our journey and share some things that have helped us make a dream become a reality. When we say this was a dream, we mean it! It wasn`t something that was even possible for either of us to believe could be part of our reality.

I (Boris) came from a very poor family. The table was poor, but it always had food and that felt like a big thing. I ended up having to get a job when I was sixteen at the local gas station. That was also the year that my mom died, and I realized that I wasn`t going to live like this. I wanted to make my mom proud and live a different type of life.

I have always loved freedom and a nine to five job wasn`t what I wanted for my life. I valued working in my own style and what I considered the best way. I have always loved working with people. Back in 2010, I was invited to attend a business seminar. After six months, I went full time into network marketing. I haven`t looked back since! I have been full time in network marketing since then and I love it!

After I (Marina) graduated from high school, I went to Switzerland and helped run a hotel there. I was satisfied with my job but there were many ups and downs with my life. The nine to five job I had wasn`t giving me what I wanted in my personal life, but it was what everyone else was doing ,and it just seemed like what I would do forever. It was hard, though, because I was missing my friends and family and didn`t really have a personal life. I just knew that I was missing out on my own freedom. I met with my friend about network marketing and didn`t really get it. I attended a meeting a couple of days later and it clicked. I stayed up all night thinking about the business and how I was ready and I was going to do whatever it took to get to the top.

We both feel incredibly blessed to have network marketing in our lives. We love the freedom that it has given us and best of all, we love that we get to work together. As you read this book and this chapter, we hope that you will start to see that your dream really can be your reality if you do the work and keep your eye focused on the vision for your future.

We have several tips and tools to share with you. These are things that we used personally to build our successful network marketing business, and they are the things that we share with our own team to help them succeed.

Tip #1 Have to have clear goals. You have to set your goals to measure your performance. Create a vision board. We love vision boards and use them ourselves all the time. We have been working on our vision board for a couple of years. When the year is finishing we look at our board and almost always we have accomplished everything that we had on our board. Only once did we not complete something within the year, and we accomplished it a couple of weeks later. We have been able to live in our dream house. Just a few weeks ago, we created our new vision board and we are excited to watch all of the things on there being accomplished.

Tip #2 You need to know your why. Knowing your emotional reason for doing this business is important. People don`t buy what you do, they buy WHY you do it. It simply shows what you believe. There will always be obstacles in your way. Your why has to be stronger than your excuses. There are days that neither of us wants to work or there is a task that is hard. Knowing our why both collectively and individually helps us to do the work anyway and get to the next task or next level in our business. Know your why and keep it top of mind.

Coaches Notes: In the last several years, I have seen these two in action. I have heard them speak in several countries and watched their growth. They both had very CLEAR goals. This may seem like a simple tip but if you want to achieve massive success, you will need to get those clear goals. You will have setbacks. You will have trials. You will have struggles that are harder than you thought they would be. If you are a conqueror, like I talk about in The Game of Conquering, you will only overcome them if you are CLEAR on your goals. To become crystal clear on your goals you will need to connect with your emotional reason. It is very hard to be clear on your goals on day one. Get as clear as you can and then keep improving that clarity so that you can become bulletproof.

Tip #3 Be careful who you surround yourself with. One of the lessons we have both learned is that you can improve your life by looking at who you are surrounding yourself with. These people that you look up to and do things with matter the most. You may need to stop hanging out with your buddies every single weekend if you find that they are all stuck doing the same thing day in and day out. The people that we surround ourselves with have a HUGE impact on how you show up in your life, and especially in your business.

We had two major things that held us back. We had the fear of failure and the fear of rejection that were big obstacles for us in this business. We as humans are naturally attached to the outcome. We think the outcome means something about us. Too much excitement or getting too down on yourself shows a lack of confidence in front of prospective clients. When we could stay focused on our why, it helped, so we kept our perspective in play all of the time and didn't let the fear hold us back.

Tip #4 The fortune is in the follow-up. People can't measure their success if they aren't following up. You cannot expect better results unless you are following up. Only 2 percent of people join with their first exposure. If you are not following up with someone, we guarantee that someone else will. One of the tools that we love to use in follow up is questions. Learn to ask a question in follow-up and then do this.... Listen. You have two ears and one mouth. Learn how to use your ears. The questions that they are asking you about the product or the opportunity are ultimately the answer.

There is a misconception that this is easy money and that they will be rich next month. The truth is this business is work! It is going to be hard work for at least three to five years in order for you to see the rewards of this business. Give yourself the gift of time in this business.

Inconsistency and procrastination. Stop avoiding the things that need to be done. It is the death of your business. Understand why you are procrastinating and work on it.

People have low self-esteem. Your posture and your esteem is important in your business. That energy is felt by others around you. Practice positive self-affirmations. It is something we both do daily. Start to focus on the small wins that you are having, while you are dreaming big. Never take a yes or a no personally.

Tip #5 Our favorite recruiting tool is our lifestyle! We always have people ask us, "What do you do?" We teach people on our team to do the same. Use your lifestyle to show people the benefits of network marketing. We teach our team how to be themselves and be unique. We teach them to not be Spamela Anderson. People want to follow people who have a good lifestyle, and they want to come. You can build a relationship with the audience. People do business with people they know, like, and trust. You must be branding yourself, not just the company. That is why this is the best way to brand yourself. Step up and become a leader that people are looking for.

Coaches Notes: People are attracted to the lifestyle you have. Social media is meant to be used to create value. When people are buying into joining your business they are buying into an aspect of your life or a leader in your team`s lifestyle. Find ways on social media to show others what this business has done for you. If you haven`t yet had success, find other ways to show what this business has done for the lifestyle of leaders on your team. Find ways to show your goals and dreams that will eventually come through this business. Sure people will judge you. They will judge no matter what though. Stop putting your dreams down to make others feel comfortable. Stop playing small. Marina and Boris had those clear goals and dreams. They sold the lifestyle they were both creating and the lifestyle they wanted to create.

Tip #6 Learn to use the tools you have around you. There
are 2.7 billion active users on Facebook worldwide. It is the largest social network in the world. Facebook and Instagram have become a modern day resume. You can reach out to more people and find your tribe. You can get your message out to more people. At the same time you are molding your audience and followers. Social media is a tool. It is a tool that can help you connect with people all over the world. If you aren`t using it in your business, you must start.

Another tool we love online is we have a broadcast list on WhatsApp of potential customers. You can add all your contacts into this broadcast. The more people you add, the more success you will have. Always send the same script to the contacts. It can be testimonials. You are going to invite those people that show interest in what you are doing to the very next online presentation. You then create a three-way chat group with those who participate in the call and also add your upline or mentor. They will help you close the prospect. We have had huge success with this.

Within the team we are doing zoom presentations for two weeks. We do five presentations a day. You have to drive the masses to see and hear about your business. From the masses you can find the people. In the third week, we have the leaders do training with new members on how to get the business started.

These are three tools we use to really help our business grow. The other thing these tools help us with is staying connected and engaged with our team and prospect. We love to have people feel like they belong, and feel the energy of this business. We saw all of the people that were excited and what they were creating with their lives. We want to do that for our people as well.

Tip #7 Be bold and learn to listen to your mentor. When your mentor makes a step forward, you need to be bold and take a step forward. Keep it simple. People love the simple things, and they are all for following the simple set up. Read as much as you can from books that will lift you and make you a better person.

Reading more will help you create a stronger positive mindset. You need to clarify the values that you live by and take responsibility for living by them. Your success is your own. It does not depend on anyone else but you. The circumstances may be tough, but what are you going to do about it? The main struggle is that everyone is excited to start the business until they go to make their first call to their friends. Have a mentor next to you that will show you how to do that first call.

When joining the business, don`t just look for a company. Look for a person that can help you set yourself up for success. Choose your mentor wisely.

Your first goal when you start your business should be to get the attention of a big leader in the company. With that I don`t mean the attention by complaining, whining, or bothering someone. You want to get their attention from having a positive posture and by your action.

Mentors shape your perspective and can fast track your success. You have to have a high teachability. You need to always be ready to listen and be teachable when your mentor gives you their time. If you have a great mentor, listen to what they are telling you, and take massive action. Invest in yourself, as well.

BONUS TIP- Working in the business as a couple is one of the biggest reasons we love this business. We complement each other in this business. Our team has spread to over 30 plus countries and has almost 80k members in less than five years because we are doing this together. We could have never done this individually. We are so different, but similar. Boris has always been a high energy numbers person, while Marina is best at inviting and sharing the products.

We attract more families doing this business together because couples see us working together and want to do that as well. We believe in the support of spouses. It is necessary to educate your spouse about this business. It is not always easy to put all of the time and energy into the business when your spouse is so negative about what you are doing. If you have an unsupportive spouse, you must decide how to proceed with the lack of support. We believe that two people that have the same vision, success is inevitable. After all, who wants to be married to a dream stealer or someone who tells you what you can and can`t do. When we started working as a couple, we started to see so many people start to have their spouse join them in the business.

This business will change you in the best way possible if you will let it. We became so much better people because of this business. We care about our health, the food we put into our bodies, and started working out because of this business. We are both more positive people because of this business. We have a better understanding of people which contributes to better relationships. This is the only business that lets you earn more the more people you help. We hope that you see what a noble business this is and do us all proud as you find your journey to financial freedom.

Coaches Notes: The world LOVES BOLDNESS! It makes people curious. It is contagious. True wealth is ability, not what you have in the bank. In order to go to the next level find a mentor, whether that be someone inside of your company or even outside of your company. I first met Boris and Marina from generic network marketing events. They were being bold, getting outside of their comfort zones and focusing on learning from other mentors. Find a mentor and be bold in doing what they teach you. You know that to get something different you are going to need to do something different. A mentor will give you the path to help you find your boldness, but in the end, it is always up to YOU. You must take action.

Author: Natalie Meek

- Car Recipient
- Top Recruiter
- Six-Figure Earner
- Multi-Million Dollar Team Leader

"The secret of getting ahead is getting started."

— Mark Twain

Part of being successful in this industry starts at the very beginning of your business; we call it launching. You want to be able to launch yourself into the business. Launch your way to recruiting. And ultimately, launch your way to success.

GET READY TO LAUNCH

Launching properly is so important. This is the introduction of your business to your network. This will be your followers first impression of your new venture and it can make or break your business. You want to pique their interest enough so they will want to come back and see what you are launching.

One of the first things required to build your brand and create a following is networking with others. Ask your friends and followers for referral posts in exchange for products from your company or other fun items. Referrals are a great way to get yourself in front of people you otherwise would not have the opportunity to meet.

You may hear it all the time, but share, share, share! It works! Launching your business means you are going to talk to a lot of people and build a lot of relationships. You have to put yourself in front of people to grow your business. Think of this analogy; if your mouth is closed your business is closed. If you are not talking to people about your business, no one will think you are serious about it or even worse, they may think you are not doing it anymore. So, talk about it! Show your excitement and people will want to know what the excitement is all about.

Coaches Notes: Get passionate as Natalie says because when you are on fire, people are either attracted to that fire or they will come to watch you burn. Either way, they are coming to watch and listen to you. Whether you are launching or relaunching your business, these same principles Natalie is teaching apply. Not only will you want to learn them for yourself, but you will want to use them to properly launch your new and future team members.

Don`t just work on growing your network to recruit, build relationships. This is so important. This is a relationship business... people join people; people relate to people, not companies, not products, they are joining because of YOU.

Attend all conventions and training events whenever possible. These events help you develop relationships with sidelines and other people within your company which essentially can end up being a huge part of your business and your network.

No matter what, keep growing your network. This can be in person or via social media platforms. This has been essential for my business. The more people you are in front of, the more people you are able to introduce your business to. This has been key for me, and I have made so many great friends in my journey.

Systems To Launch

In my business, by following the steps I have listed below I was able to grow a team of over 5,000 women. I coached and led my team to duplicate these steps which resulted in considerable growth. Duplication is such a huge part of this business. If we can make things simple for team members coming into the business, they will be more successful and more likely to stay with your company.

1. *Schedule a meeting with your upline.* This is a great time for you to learn a little more about the business, the products, and to go over your company's fast start program. During this time, create a game plan to achieve your fast start.

2. *Find your "Why."* Establishing a why is extremely important in this industry because if you do not have a reason why you are doing this, not only are you less likely to take your business seriously, but you are more likely to give up. It will also help your upline know how much to help and push you towards your goals.

3. *It's time to create a BUZZ...Your First Social Media Post.* Share your excitement and make a public announcement post or video on Facebook Live! It's time to let everyone you know that you are doing something new and exciting. It is essential that you DO NOT WAIT UNTIL YOUR KIT ARRIVES TO DO THIS! You do not need the product to promote your business. If doing a post instead of a video, I highly recommend posting a picture of yourself looking excited; this will grab people's attention. This is basically your chance to do a 'teaser' post to get people to follow your posts. You don't have to go into detail about everything, you just want to peek interest with your followers so they will continue to watch you.

EXAMPLE "Teaser" POST

HOLY MOLY...you guys. I think I found the (insert product) JACKPOT! I have found so many awesome (industry) products and can't contain my excitement! This one has got to be my favorite so far... (INSERT PRODUCT!!!!) It is so easy and IS AMAZING!! Who else needs this like... NOW?! Stay tuned! I am going to post more about this soon!!! (Insert video or selfie.)

4. *Promoting the Product.* Once your kit arrives consider doing an unboxing video on Facebook Live. If you are not comfortable doing a Facebook Live, consider doing a selfie of you holding your kit with all your new products. Show your excitement in whatever you choose to do and just be YOU! You'll be surprised at the response.

5. *Follow Up Post.* Do another post or Facebook Live about how much you love the products after using them. You should do this within a day or two of getting your kit. This will generate a buzz and your followers will be interested!

6. *Opportunity Post.* Create a post about the flood of messages you are receiving regarding your new company and the amazing new products. In the post, ask your followers if they are searching for something fun and exciting and if they think your product is as fabulous as you do. Let them know how simple and easy this is and that you can show them how you did it!

7. *Fortune is in the FOLLOW UP!* Remember, you're building relationships and your brand. Make sure you are replying to each and every comment on your posts or Facebook Lives and that you are responding to your followers in a private message.

Coaches Notes: These 7 steps give you the strategy to LAUNCH your business and launch your new team members. Launching a business is like a new movie release. When a new movie launches well it makes a huge difference. It creates momentum and confidence. Don`t stress if you didn`t launch very well. That is why I keep referring back to relaunching yourself and launching your new future team members. Follow Natalie`s 7 step guide and adapt it to your company. Adapt it to your style and crush your relaunch/launch.

When I started this business I was coming from an insurance sales background. I loved my job, but I knew there was no way I was going to be able to walk away from my sweet son after only six weeks. I needed time to be with our growing family and more money to provide the things we would need moving forward.

I knew I was a hard worker; I have always been a hustler. I jumped in with both feet and joined a Network Marketing company! I had no idea what I was doing, but the rush and excitement I felt from that experience was amazing and that is when I knew I was hooked! I loved Network Marketing!

Failure To Launch

Early in my Network Marketing career, I was afraid to share my business. I was afraid of what people would think of me doing network marketing. I remember being scared to even post on my social media accounts. One day, I realized that the people who may judge me do not pay my bills, so why am I afraid of what they think? I don`t know why I let that hold me back, but I think this feeling is so common in this industry and it keeps so many people from being successful. This is not a career you should be ashamed of. It is a career you should be proud of because it creates more millionaires than any other industry out there. Once I started to truly open up, my business exploded. Do not be afraid to tell people what you do, be proud to share with them. If you are not talking about what you do, the doors to your business may as well be closed. The truth is, you never know whose life you just might change by sharing your opportunity with them.

I know that my fear of other people`s opinions is a common fear that many people have. There are so many other things that hold people back. It is important to know what some of them are, so you don`t find yourself using them as an excuse to not work or even worse, quit. People sometimes think this is a get rich quick kind of thing and it`s just not. Oftentimes I see people get frustrated because they don`t see instant success, but this is a business that takes a lot of time, hard work, and dedication to be successful. You will get out of your business what you put in it. I always tell my team, if you treat it like a hobby, you will make a hobby paycheck.

Lack of Confidence. This is a big one. You have to be confident in yourself and your products because if you`re not, people will see that. You also cannot be scared to post on social media. Remember what I said earlier...these people do not pay your bills, don`t forget that.

Consistency. You MUST stay consistent with working your business. This means doing incoming producing activities each and every day. If you aren`t working your business, you cannot expect it to grow. I had to stay consistent with my business. Growing in network marketing didn`t happen for me overnight.

Every year, every company was a learning experience and stepping stone that got me that much closer to being home with my family and to the leader I wanted and knew I could be. Take the time to attend training events, read self development books, participate in all your corporate and team training. Personal development has been a huge key to my success.

Network Marketing has done so much for my family. It has kept me home with my now three children for nearly 12 years. I am able to work when I want to, not when I have to. It has enabled my family to have more and truly live a life we can enjoy. Before network marketing, we struggled financially like so many families out there. Life was just harder and there is no way we would have been able to provide for our children the way we do today had I never taken that leap of faith 12 years ago. Network Marketing has changed everything for us and it can change everything for you too if you really want it to.

Don`t hold back. Be yourself and make sure you are putting your product and your opportunity in front of your audience. Remember to build relationships because people don`t join companies; people join people, so show your audience the real YOU. Mix it up and make sure you are putting content out that has value and shows who you are. Post content that makes them want to come back and see what you will post next. If you are having a hard time figuring out what to do. Start here. Start in this book with this chapter and take one thing you have learned and apply it today. Be consistent and you will be amazed at what you can create.

Coaches Notes: The sooner you can learn from Natalie`s and my mistake of worrying way too much what everyone else thinks the better. Most of us fear the judgment of others. Most of us care way too much about the opinions of those who don`t pay our bills. Natalie went to another level when she stopped worrying about what everyone else thought. When we let our EGO go and focus on helping others we give ourselves permission for success.

Author: Anthony Napolitano

- Featured in Forbes, Yahoo Finance, ABC, And many more...

- Number one earner in his company

- Was inducted into the network marketing pro hall of fame at twenty four years old!

"Winners do what winners do!"

Sports have always been a huge part of my life growing up. I didn`t have a vision of being a lawyer or doctor. I always had a vision of being a professional athlete. I was blessed to have great athletic ability, and in high school, I played baseball and basketball. I got into a major university and started to pursue my baseball career. The goal was to go pro and live my life as a professional baseball player.

That year I started playing at the collegiate level, I got a wake-up call. I saw some of the guys I played with and other friends graduate with massive amounts of debt, no job, and some were moving back in with their parents. I started to wonder what I would do if I got hurt or if something prevented me from being a pro baseball player. I didn`t have a fallback plan. I knew the 9-5 life was not for me, but if the pro career didn`t work out, what would I do?

I started to do research on entrepreneurship as a whole. I wanted to know what some of the most successful people in the world did to create their own wealth. They owned businesses and they had their money work for them. They have leverage. Leverage is the key to wealth. I had to create leverage, but I had no money, and no experience, and no idea how to even start creating leverage.

I believe everything happens for a reason, and that same year, I met a guy at a college party that wasn`t going to college. He seemed interesting and we connected on Instagram. He shot me a DM a couple of days later and told me he was working on something big that he thought I would be great at. That is how I got exposed to network marketing. I was so skeptical. He sent a message after, and said, "I think we can make a lot of money together." That didn`t help the skepticism! But I checked him out on social media. He was driving a fancy car and lived in a beautiful home. He was doing something right. I decided to put my ego aside for a second and met up with him. I haven`t looked back since and that was seven years ago.

I became a six-figure earner within the first twelve months. I did it all while going to school and playing sports. It was a part-time thing for me. I went from making six to seven figures three years in. I was making more money than any of my friends or family and I had to decide if I wanted to keep going to school, or if I wanted to start to really make this my thing and go all in. I was putting consistent hours in but hadn't gone all in.

> **Coaches Notes:** I need to start out by pointing out something very important. Anthony is one of the highest-earning millennials in all of network marketing. Let me also point out he works as hard as anyone I know. I have heard countless times that millennials don't work ... Anthony has all ages on his team, but he has found a huge group of millennials that see the same vision Anthony has. The main point is that each demographic, country and gender have different weaknesses but they also have huge strengths. You truly get what you are looking for. Anthony refused to believe that all millennials don't work and instead found so many hard working millennials. It all started with his work ethic and vision. He will talk about that vision here in this next part.

Be Coachable And Have Vision

There are two things that network marketing comes down to. Coachability and vision. That`s it. Everything else you can learn over time. You have the time. Network marketing is not a difficult concept but it takes work. Some people say it is easy. It`s not easy. It is a simple business that takes effort and work. It is easy to learn. It will take a couple of weeks to master the system.

I came in and knew that I didn`t know what I was doing. I went in with my mentors and was coachable. I wanted to soak up everything they said. I didn`t question what they were asking me to do, I just went in and did it. Some people want to question things and make it harder on themselves. I told my mentor, you know what you are doing, show me.

I didn`t have any experience. I had never had a job. I have never filled out a W-2 form in my life. So I was inexperienced but extremely coachable. I didn`t know anything. Be coachable and willing to learn and you can do it. When I talk about being coachable, I mean being willing to listen to people that have walked the road before you. Know that your mentor has some valuable things to tell you, but you have to be willing to listen and pay attention.

Use Your Words Wisely

Everything is lingo. It is what you say. Too often people aren`t looking and thinking about their words. Everything in network marketing is related. You have to be willing to relate to people. You should be able to put anything in a text and make it be something that your prospect can relate to. I use a lot of examples and metaphors because it helps people relate.

There is a saying that goes, "If you ask for money, you will get opinions. If you ask for opinions, you will get money." It means if you tell people they can make a ton of money in this business, you will get all of their opinions. If you ask for their opinion on what you have going on, people will give it to you, and that is how you get the money.

I work with a younger generation. Some of them won`t even know what network marketing is. So how do you describe it when they ask, "What is network marketing?" Remember, to make it relate to them. I say something like, "You know how when you download an app and they tell you they will give you money if you refer your friends to the app? That is what network marketing is. That is what we do here." Make it easy to make sense in their mind.

So many people are not relating to the audience. You have to relate it to the person you are talking to. Figure out their problem and how you are going to be a problem solver for them. Your opportunity or product is a solution to your problem. You have to be relatable and solve for them.

Tonality and posture is everything. When people start, they beg people to join them. Without the opportunity, they have nothing. You have the golden goose. You have an opportunity. Most people who get started have average jobs. They are working 9-5 and just getting by. Why are you begging that person when that person needs you?

Take the invite. I am offering you an invite to take a look at the opportunity. Hey, what are you doing tonight at 7:00pm ET? They answer back, "I`m free, what`s up?" I say, "I would love to get your opinion on something. It`s 7:00 pm ET and it`s mostly visual. I would love for you to take a look and get your opinion about it."

That is simple. If they rebuttal and say What is it?" It is all about posture and tonality. This is huge with the rebuttal, "It is 90 percent visual. I am not going to get into it over the phone, I don`t want to ruin the experience for you. If you can`t make it, no big deal. I have two other people interested, and I only have two spots available. If you can`t make it, I can move on to them." Take away the opportunity from them. It is all about posture and tonality. How do you carry yourself? You can`t waver if someone says no to you or questions you. People follow a leader.

I train my team that once someone has done the presentation they follow up and say, "Let`s get you started." That`s it. Don`t make it complicated.

Don`t ask people what they think. It can go really good or really bad. Don`t take a 50/50 chance. Posture yourself to make the sale. If they rebuttal, then you can have the conversation.

From a meeting book a meeting. If they tell me they don`t have the money, I ask them what day they get paid. If they say, Friday I ask them, "OK what time on Friday can we get together to get you started?" Always plan the next event. If you tell them they can come back to you when they do have the money, a lot of things are going to get in your way of getting that money. The jobs, the kids, the girlfriends. These are the things you need to understand. It is the few words that make the difference. How are you positioning yourself to change your words and make the sale.

Five Step System

teach the simplest five-step system. It only takes twenty minutes to learn this and anyone can go out and make money.

Step 1 80 percent of people are just customers. They are happy paying customers. For them to fall in love with it, you have to have them using it quickly. Get it in their hands, and get them using it.

Step 2 Make a list. If you don`t have people, you don`t have a business. If McDonald`s doesn`t have burgers and fries, they don`t have a business. You need people. Make the list of your people. Network marketing is a people business, so go out and get the people.

Step 3 Master the invite. Be the preview, not the movie. You are just connecting dot A to dot B. You can`t explain everything right out of the gate. You can`t give them all of the details. You don`t have to. Your job is to invite. Connect people that can close the deals for you.

Step 4 Edify. You have to let people know who they are talking to. You have to put importance on the speaker and on the company. Edify the business and the person doing the presentation. They don`t want to talk to an average Joe. You may not have the experience yet to be a mentor figure for them. You want to give them someone to look up to that can be that mentor figure.

Step 5 Follow up. From a meeting book a meeting. 99 percent of people have never done sales in their life. We have to show people how to follow up and get organized. Most people miss the business because they aren`t following up.

Simple. I have duplicated off of this. So many people make this so confusing. People want to have success. They want instant gratification. Keep it simple so that they can come in and get a taste for success.

Coaches Notes: The #1 cause of failure is indecision. The top leaders always stick to a simple system. The non-successful distributors complicate everything and lack focus. Follow either Anthony`s simple five step system or find a system that works for you but find one. Once you find that system now, you can focus on everything to better execute it. Now you can become obsessed with doing the basics better. Now you can master the mundane and crush your business.

Play The Long Game

I thought even if I didn`t succeed in the first five years, it wouldn`t be a problem. If I could set myself up for not worrying about money, it would be worth it, even if it took me a while to figure it out. I could do what I want, when I want. It would be worth it. I adopted that quickly, and I teach others that. It is a game changer for the younger generation.

I got so many no`s in the beginning. I had hundreds of no`s the first couple of weeks. I had such ambition. The no didn`t bother me, because I thought to myself, "no big deal. I will be doing this a very long time." It didn`t discourage me.

If people are just trying it out they get discouraged very quickly. They don`t see the long game, and they quit. The twenty year mentality made the difference for me and the members of my team that have adopted it. By staying on that even keel and not getting too high or too low is awesome.

It is not hard to build momentum when things are going well. The thing that really shows your business mindset is what you do in those downtimes. My philosophy is that I am even head on your shoulders.

Look at the athletes that are most successful. When you look at them you can`t tell if they are winning big or losing big. Because they always know that the next game is coming. Most people are looking at the result they are currently looking at. They stop their activity based on their emotion. When your business is in downtime, can you sustain your momentum enough to make it to the next goodtime. That is what creates success in network marketing. Most people don`t hold it together. They let it fall over all the way down and then essentially start over every six months. Someone leaves their team, and they wallow there and let their business fail, then they build again and wonder why it feels so hard. They didn`t maintain the momentum. It is a never ending process.

Consistent activity is what matters. It isn`t what you do during the good times, but your consistent activity during the bad times that create your success. I make more money every single year. When people ask me how I have been able to do it, I tell them. I have no emotional attachment to this business. Good day, bad day, I take them all. I am getting on calls, I am traveling. No matter what is going on I am not letting my emotions affect my consistency. During the good times, I grow extremely fast. During the bad times sustain. It is an endless cycle and I show up consistently through it all. It is a nice stock chart. It will keep going up over time!

Be more logical than emotional. Look at some of the most successful companies you see today. Apple, Amazon, Dyson to name a few. These were failing businesses for ten years. You have to have vision for what is to come. Don`t let emotions in the moment take your momentum.

Play The Game

For me the business was just another sport. I grew up and sports was everything. I went to school, came home did homework, and went to practice. That was my life. It was school and sports. Sports were my life. Travel, everything I ever did was about sports. So when I got into network marketing it was just another sport. I focused on the sport of it. I knew the money would come when the skills were there. So many people focus on the money and they miss it.

It is always a game. We are about to beat another company record this week. It is a game. All of the team is part of this competitiveness and game. If you aren't having fun in this industry, then you are in the wrong business. This is a fun industry. Love what you do, and play the game. At the end of the day, I would tell people, stay with it. You may not be in the place you want to be in right now, but stay with it, anyway.

Everyone that is still in the industry that I can remember from seven years ago and has stuck with it is massively successful. Play the long game. The people that stick and play make money. Stay consistent with it, and you will have the success you desire. This is a sport. It is just fun. Stay committed to yourself and play the best game you can.

Coaches Notes: Anthony simplified and focused. Anthony created a vision and then went to work. He played the long game by marrying the process and divorcing the results. Very few do this. And even less do this at a young age. Anthony was so committed to his vision he created a contagious energy that led a movement. Don't make this business so complicated. As you notice time and time again with each one of the leaders in this book .... They all keep it really simple and focus on the execution, but it always begins with the right mindset. What are you doing to improve your mindset on a DAILY BASIS? Check out some more tips on improving your mindset at www.sperrybonus.com

Author: Rhiannon Neuharth

- International Speaker and Leader

- Two time published author

- Podcast & Blog contributor

- Founder of the "90 Day Sprint"

- Five hundred thousand dollar+ industry earner

- Earned trips and cars

- Homeschool Mom

- Former Middle/High Science Teacher

You can do everything wrong with the right attitude and succeed, or you can do everything right with the wrong attitude and fail."

-Author Unknown

Learn To Be Led

first joined network marketing when I was 18. I had NO idea what I was doing, but I caught the vision of what it could do for my future. I had watched my Mom as a kid in the same company and had grown up using the products. Like many joined for a discount and didn`t work it as a business. Time passed, and I decided I wanted to truly give this industry a try. I hated having a boss so being told what to do and when I could see friends or family was not something I wanted for the rest of my life.

The second time I joined the same company, I was committed to working as a business, not a hobby. I was older and truly wanted to unlock the vision of freedom and flexibility I knew was possible for myself and my future family. My upline was a family friend I had grown up with, so I felt comfortable partnering with and getting advice from her. She stretched me, encouraged me, and found me a local mentor to tap into. I credit SO much personal growth to this part of my life and to her belief in me.

At this point in my life I was very shy. I had never been the person in high school that was popular, most of my friends were GUYS (I was selling makeup), I had been over weight and was extremely self-conscious. To top it off I didn`t even WEAR makeup!! I was the least likely person you would ever think would be successful. Since my sponsor was across the country, she partnered me with a local leader to help me find my way.

I would watch her connect with prospects while I hid behind coat racks terrified and listened. Eventually with both of their encouragement, I eased out of my comfort zone and over time, it became part of who I am today. Eventually I connected with another mentor that was well recognized in the company and I sat in on many three-way calls, inventory talks, etc., until I started doing them on my own. I showed up every week to meetings consistently. With her guidance, I excelled quickly and earned a company car and broke into leadership ranks in the company.

Unfortunately, the title and car did not come with the sustainable paycheck I needed. I ended up returning the car and leaving the company a few months later while finishing my last year of college. I was embarrassed, devastated and at 25 just two months before getting married filed for bankruptcy. At that point, I swore off the industry with a "never again" attitude... little did I know God had other plans.

When my husband and I flew to Mexico to get married just a month after my bankruptcy was finalized, we met a couple on their honeymoon. Naturally, we became Facebook friends and kept in touch.

About a year and a half later, I saw a before and after of her post momma belly results from a product she had tried. Like any new Mom, my belly was squishy and I hated how it made me feel. I was shocked by her results and eventually reached out to her. She shared what she was using and about the income potential, and I was excited but nervous. Rightfully so, my husband was absolutely NOT on board after the last sour experience. He told me I could do what I wanted (I am more of an ask for forgiveness than permission kind of person) but I wanted him involved in this new adventure. I filled out the enrollment application online three times before finally hitting submit. To say I was terrified is an understatement.

At that time we were robbing Peter to pay Paul, and although we were both working, we didn`t have any extra money. Our first home purchase had multiple unknown problems causing us to sink what little we had into major repairs. Additionally, my daughter was chronically ill, and no one could tell us why. It felt like one thing after another. There was no other option but to find something I could work around my job and caring for a child with extra needs. We needed to bring in some additional income and give us some breathing room and this was the best option. The days I missed teaching to be home with her meant a smaller paycheck. I had to decide between being a Mother that should be home nurturing her sick child, or working to put food on the table. The endless battle of Mom-guilt was AWFUL. I felt like no matter what I did, I was failing. I had to make a decision to give it my all or continue to stay stuck, tired and broke. One day, my school directress mocked me about my attendance due to my daughter's health and told me to go "sell that thing". It fired me up and forced me to commit to leaving a job that cared so little about me and my child's desperate health situation!

Once I committed to proving her wrong, it was sink or swim. From my experience, people are motivated by inspiration or desperation, and for me it was certainly desperation. I was desperate to be home with my daughter and fought relentlessly until I was able to make it happen.

That first six months included very little sleep and a lot of hard work. For months, I would do at least 1 vendor event per month and hold appointments on weekends. I took no days off between work and my business. Every day after school, the little time I had was consumed by holding a daily power hour. This consisted of phone calls to book appointments from leads at the events, follow up calls, or networking within the community. From those daily calls, I would book 8-10 appointments every weekend. Immediately after, I would rush to pick up my son from Montessori and the nightly chaos began. Feeding and bathing two children under three, getting them in bed while my husband worked his evening retail job, all before collapsing into bed. Instead of a much-needed night`s rest, I would be up all night listening to my daughter scream in pain. It was an exhausting cycle, I wondered if it would ever end.

If you are struggling with a difficult situation in your life while building your business remember this: YOU can do ANYTHING for a short period of time when it results in a long-term gain.

Coaches Notes-I know Rhiannon very well personally from personal coaching and masterminds. Rhiannon knows the value of investing in herself and coming to masterminds. I know her story and still after reading it, I relearn the power of stories and sacrifice. Here is the problem with network marketing. Unlike a traditional business where the investment can be very large, it is relatively small. Due to this small investment, people TRY network marketing. They don`t DO IT! Their financial sacrifice is so small that they give up easier than one would with a traditional business. Can you imagine investing $50,000 into a traditional business only to quit within a few months? It is unfathomable, because it wouldn`t happen. You would fight to make it work. Rhiannon had a huge sacrifice because of the situation she was in. She used that desperation to her advantage to dig deep and crush her business.

The next lesson is the power of storytelling. You have probably heard the saying, "facts tell and stories sell." People are more and more skeptical these days with the bombardment of advertising. Stories are the most relatable, authentic way to attract others to your business and products. LEARN to tell your story. You may not think you have a great story, but I promise you that you do. We all do. You just need to learn to tell it.

Be Driven To Succeed

I remember one specific day when I was EXHAUSTED. No sleep, no breaks, and the kids were crying for me as I headed for the door to my appointments for the day. I glanced at my husband with the look of sheer exhaustion. He had a screaming baby on his hip and a sad toddler at his feet. Everyone was surrounding the door as I tried to slip out. With exhaustion on my face and in my voice, I said, "I have to go." He responded, "Just go," tired and exasperated himself. At that moment I felt like a terrible Mom and Wife. I wanted a day off. A break. The entire way to my first appointment, I questioned myself and what I was doing. But I did it anyway, because my WHY was my kids. It was being home with my daughter. It was being able to take care of her and no longer missing doctor appointments, surgeries or having to leave her with a sitter just to put food on the table.

Many nights I sat in the recliner in her room holding her at 2 am and 3 am so she could sleep while sending Facebook messages following up with prospects. Ironically this chair now sits in my office. Lots of business can be done in off hours, so do not let your availability hinder your success. Don`t give yourself an option to quit.

At the time, my goal was to get to $4,000 in commissions a month to quit my teaching job. It was plastered on my bathroom mirror on a sticky note with another that said, "Don`t think, just do." That was the line I had to cross to make being home with her a reality. It was what FUELED me and would allow me to take care of her. To put her and my family first. I made sacrifices to get what I wanted and needed long term without sacrificing my integrity, and still do to this day. Sleep and a bit of sanity were two others. This is what continues to push me to become the leader I am today.

You may not start out envisioning being a leader, I know I didn`t! Remember, I was the least likely person to be pegged as the "type" to be a leader (or successful) when I started network marketing. You may be an accidental leader, meaning your team has grown simply because you are excited! Just know, not enough people are committed to the process, to the mistakes, consistency, and growth that it takes when pursuing a goal and long-term success. I absolutely could have let my past failures hold me back, derail me, or keep me from trying. I could have let my daughter`s health stop me from achieving my goal of being home with her. I just kept going back to the vision of what I KNEW this industry could and would do for our family, so I HAD to keep going. It was the only option.

Be Coachable, You Don't Know It All!

I know it is scary, especially if you have extenuating circumstances like I did, but you MUST be committed and go all in knowing that you have a mentor there to help you learn. If you don't have a direct upline to work with, connect with someone that resonates with you! ASK for their help. As the saying goes, "When the student is ready, the teacher appears." Be willing to listen and do what they offer and make mistakes. So often I see people wade through this industry and dabble without commitment. They don't need it enough or they fail to commit to learning the process. They don't ever fully dive in and learn and grow, simply giving up because it's easier than failing forward. CONFIDENCE comes through CONSISTENCY!

Coachability is essential to success. No one starts knowing what they are doing, most start this industry and do not ever plan to become a leader-it happens by default simply by sharing what you love! You may have some skills or training that you have obtained but acquiring skills for this industry is a process that is developed over time. You have to be willing to take constructive feedback and apply it. Not argue about it or think about. Apply IT. My motto is "Don't think, just do." DO what your mentor says, even if you feel weird. The more you do something, the easier it becomes and the more natural it is in your routine. I want to encourage you to take the actions right away and don't let fear or objections hold you back. It is the people that take the action the fastest that see results fastest. You just have to be willing to work consistently and be coachable as you go.

Starting out in this industry can be overwhelming, but it is important to remember to take it one day at a time. I am still learning after over a decade. The great thing about it is that you don`t have to know it all to start. Let me be clear, this is not a comfortable process. You probably gathered how insecure I was when I started. I one hundred percent believe that if I had not joined this industry, I would not have gone to teaching. At that time, I didn`t have the confidence to stand up in front of groups and speak, let alone speak on stages across the world. If you are willing to be led, stretch and grow, you can become successful in any area of this industry. Had my first mentor not invited me to watch her, then gently nudge me and encourage me, I would not have accomplished the things I have and continue to do.

Think back to when you joined your company. What was the immediate need that you had that made you want to start this business? This is an essential piece to know about yourself and the people you are recruiting. When people are driven in this business from the start, it comes from their immediate needs. You always hear "If your why makes you cry"... it sounds so corny, but it is the truth. You have to have PURPOSE, and the VISION will come. When you know where you are going and why, others want to come with you!

Sometimes people go and do their own thing and get frustrated because they are not seeing the results they are looking for right away. Often, this happens because they have an "I can do this better than you" attitude. Sadly, a majority of those people do not last long due to lack of coachability. Often they simply didn`t do what they were advised to do, so leading them to think it doesn`t work. Others make an excuse that it is too hard and give up (the whiners). Some never even truly give it a try and go into the witness protection program not long after they start! From my experience there may just be a minor tweak that can make all the difference in the outcome and results of efforts.

Coaches Notes: Learn to use your excuses as the reason to have success. Every leader I know has doubted themselves at some point. Every leader I know has had times where they considered quitting. You aren`t strange for having those kinds of thoughts. There will be days where you aren`t sure if it is worth it, which is why you need to dig deep. Surround yourself with the right environment. Rhiannon created statements of positivity and put them up in her bathroom. She did personal development. She protected her energy and created an environment to support her VISION and DREAMS. My challenge for you is to clean up your environment. Create affirmations that you post in your office and or bathroom mirrors. Stick with personal development. Don`t allow the dream crushers to tell you that you can`t. Create boundaries for those dream crushers and let them know negativity is unacceptable.

What Drives You?

As you now know, people are moved by inspiration or desperation. I had to figure it out. I had to make this work for my family to survive. My husband didn't support me, my boss didn't support me... so I HAD to do this for me. To show everyone that I COULD do what I put my mind to.

Isn't it interesting that when we get put in a tough situation, somehow we always figure it out? That is when our mess becomes our message. I emphasized this to my students often instead of giving the answer, I made them think for themselves. I do this to my team as well. Their deductions are almost always exactly what they needed. All they wanted was reassurance they weren't messing up. Your new team members are the exact same! Nurture them but do not spoon feed them! They will build their confidence through their experience. Robbing them of their independence creates codependency instead of independent business owners, you end up with a team that is not sustainable without YOU. Heaven forbid something should happen to you and your legacy falls apart.

Invest the time to figure out what is driving your prospects and team. Not everyone has the same goals as you, and you should never push your goals onto someone else. Their "why" is different than yours, and that is OK! You aren't their boss; you are their mentor. Ask questions to see their personality types and what their motivations are. Knowing personality types helps you drive them and encourage them in ways that resonate with them, their goals, and their personality. If I know I have someone that is a nurturing personality that loves to help people, we are going to utilize their personality and skills and help them build their business. If someone is driven by money or details, their reach-outs will look much different. There is NO one size fits all to building a business.

Customize your leadership but don't compromise the goal or system. Keeping the same system but modifying small tweaks with each person to help them feel more comfortable taking action is key. You can't modify EVERYTHING, but small things like scripts for reaching out are huge. Helping them feel comfortable and walking them through the process is essential, but it is still up to them to take action. Let them know you are with them each step. Give them an assignment, let them do the work and check in with you. If they do not do that, then they are either not committed or are letting fear hold them back.

As a teacher by trade, I have watched different students learn different ways. For example, I don't learn well by video. I tell one of my own personal coaches all the time that I need things typed out and printed so I can really learn. It is the best way for me and it helps me to be able to dive into the material and retain it. Since this realization, I strive to have handouts for live videos, or to keep them basic and simple so they are easy to follow and implement immediately.

We recently started a new onboarding system that has made all the difference. That includes using a simple questionnaire to get to know new team members. It asks questions about what skills they have and how they may be able to apply them, the way they learn best, how much time they want to dedicate to their business, and how quickly they want to reach their financial goal. It helps us connect on a different level- as a person with dreams and goals, not just a number in the system. It also helps you to find out what drives them-inspiration or desperation.

This is a technique that I learned while attending one of several generic events. It wasn't until the last year or so that I started to tap back into my teaching skills to help people learn a way that would work better for them. We are all different, and while I can't physically accommodate everything for everyone, I am much more conscious of visuals, handouts, etc., for training purposes in addition to step by step processes to help them grow.

Leadership Is A Verb

Leadership is not a title, it`s an action. It is a verb. It is you showing up consistently and doing the work. Don`t be confused-a title doesn`t make a leader, your actions do. The first and most important person you will lead ever is yourself. Mentoring and leading others are two totally different things. Leading is showing the way by your actions. Mentoring is inviting them in and being actively engaged in their learning. It`s support and guidance as you go. Teachers call this the gradual release method. Mentoring is inviting a team member on three-way calls and letting them shadow you like mine did in my first business. This is called the "show-tell-do method." Show them how it is done, tell them how they can do it better by giving them guidance on feedback (similar to an internship), then have them do it while connecting and providing feedback so they can improve. This is a huge piece that is missing often in this industry and causes the leadership gap. A leadership gap is when someone hits a rank and slips down to a lower rank because they do not have the skills to match their level of success. More leaders in this industry need to focus on mentorship, not just leadership.

The best thing you can do for your business today is lead yourself and mentor your newest person, even if you are only one week ahead of them! What do I mean by that? WORK YOUR BUSINESS FIRST! The great thing about this industry is you can learn AND earn at the same time! Show up, stay consistent and be someone your team can count on. As the saying goes, those that SHOW UP, GO UP! The more you show up the more you learn.

As a detail-oriented person, I wanted to know how to close, and to hear how someone invited others to do the business. I NEEDED that for my personality so I could feel comfortable and confident in what I was doing. I did exactly what my mentors did and suggested. I used my mentors as a TOOL, and I got to work implementing what I had learned. I mastered the skills because I listened in on someone who was excelling. Hearing her do it over and over again, implementing what I observed, gave me the confidence to do it myself.

Oftentimes many want the title and check without the effort and responsibility of leadership. I see many people stop taking action because they get frustrated and down on themselves instead of being willing to learn and grow. You must keep your eye on the bigger picture so you can keep learning and growing, and eventually the results will follow.

Ask yourself:

- How am I showing up for the team? Remember, it is NOT about you!! Leadership is showing up, stepping in to help where needed with or without being asked and being a team player.

- Am I doing my IPA`s (Income Producing Activities)? How often?

- Am I consistently doing the work it takes to be successful?

- Am I implementing what I learn, even if I don`t do it right the first time?

We understand that you may not be able to attend everything LIVE, but staying connected and making your business a priority if you want to see long term success as a leader is crucial.

It doesn`t matter if you have the numbers or not, show up as a leader who is willing to do the work and be accountable with your mentor. You have probably gathered by now the reiteration of coachablity. As a leader it helps to sort the wanters and the whiners. The ones that WANT success versus the ones that ask for help, never implement the coaching and whine that "it just isn`t working for them." Remember to ALWAYS stay coachable. Your growth and success depend on it.

Do You Have A Hobby Or A Business?

When people come to me frustrated about their lack of results, I ask them to show me their numbers and screen shots of their messages. When they look at me puzzled, I take time to educate them on the importance of conversations/closing and tracking your numbers. If you don`t know your numbers, you have a hobby not a business. Hobbies cost money, businesses make money. Are you doing better than you were two months ago? You won`t know if you aren`t tracking your numbers. This industry is all about the numbers and seeing patterns in your business. Maybe it is the teacher in me, but tracking has always been a huge part of what I do. It is important to know that not every month will be a huge month, there will be ebbs and flows. Hitting a rank doesn`t mean you will stay there. Tracking helps you to see what it took to GET there, so if and when you do have a slower period, you can rest assured knowing the numbers don`t lie. This topic is often omitted or overlooked, but setting the reality and expectation of leadership is essential to growth both personally and professionally.

Here are a few things I encourage you to track:

- How many did you share a 3rd party tool and follow up with?
- Bookings or appointments (my first sponsor always told me out of bookings, out of business)
- How many three-way calls did you do with an upline?
- Total enrollments (daily/monthly)
- What are your beginning and end of day volume numbers?
- Total number of enrollments for the month
- Paycheck (weekly/monthly)

By tracking my numbers every single day, I am able to see where I can improve and grow. Start to match your numbers to your company's comp plan or rank to see how much volume you will need to hit the next rank or promotion. Work backwards: Break rank goals down into daily increments to make it easier on yourself to see the possibility of achieving the goal. If you are tracking, you should be able to see the outcome and what you need to do to get to the next milestone in your business.

STAY CONNECTED and ACCOUNTABLE to your mentor by checking in DAILY with your results. They will be far more inclined to continually mentor you if you commit to this simple daily practice.

Social Skills

As we know, most network marketers build their businesses on social media. It allows you to do more in less time. Maybe you can talk to five people in person during one day. You may be able to text twenty. Connecting on social media means that you have access to millions of people every single day and the ability to never run out of leads if you take daily consistent action. It is CRUCIAL if you build online to avoid being a "spammy pammy." Share your business authentically in a way that you will draw people to you, not push them away.

It is just as important to know your stats for social media. Such as:

How many messages did you send (and what was the content of the message)? You can message people but not get the results you are looking for simply by saying the wrong thing or over-sharing. Connect with a mentor if you aren`t seeing the results with your messages. This is why tracking is so important. It helps you to see what areas you need to improve. Numbers don`t lie, but people do.

How often and what are you posting? You should not be posting tons of generic spammy posts. You are YOU first, your business is part of you but not all of who you are. When I look back at my past on social media, some of my posts were TERRIBLE! I didn`t have the likes or the comments, but I was consistent on my commenting, my engaging and posting. Content is essential, but engagement is even more important in order for more people to see your posts.

Be consistent before the likes and comments happen. Don`t compare your social equity to others! It has taken me YEARS to create the engagement I do now and knowing my audience. Knowing my audience, what to post and when. People are watching and seeing what you do. Every post matters even when there is low engagement, just don`t OVER post. If you don`t see the engagement you are looking for, post it at another time and make sure to engage with others PRIOR to posting. Figure out what your audience wants and engages with most. Social media is a tool, not a toy. Use it right, it can pay you big! It is all about presenting yourself in a way that people can get to know you (by sharing your story) and why you do what you do.

Our team has a weekly flow. We have a themed post or action for each day of the week and promote to the next event or get someone into an ATM group (add, tag, message). It all comes down to getting used to posting properly. You have to get people in that flow, because we want to get them consistent. For example, Fridays are "follow up Friday." It is part of what we do and drives duplication and simplicity for the newest recruit.

Finding the numbers you want to track and consistently tracking them will make it that much easier for you to know where your business and development needs help and support.

The Importance Of Generic Events

Generic events and masterminds are important for learning and improving skills, strategies and techniques. A generic event is an event that is held by a coach or organization that is not company specific. Before my first event, I didn`t realize how much value I would walk away with from these events. Not just the actionable items, but also the amazing connections and friendships I made. When I got back from my first event in England, I was grateful for the chance to have a place to enhance my skills, not just get hyped up like a company event. I loved it so much, I immediately booked to attend another event that happened the following month in Vegas and ended up speaking at another just two months after that with Rob and another mentor of mine.

If your leadership is not supportive of you or your business, find someone else that will mentor you. Not everyone`s personality will mesh and that is OK! Just remember, they may not have been supportive if you have not taken the coaching and implemented what was taught previously. Remember, be honest with yourself in this process. It doesn`t have to be someone in your company. There are many amazing top trainers in this industry to choose from. I have gotten so much from having a variety of coaches the last two years. It has allowed me to find what resonates with me and my goals with a different outlook and perspective. Find the support that you need, even if it is from a generic mentor. The principles remain the same, no matter the product company r service is being provided. Collaborate with others. Share what is working for you and ask for help where you need support.

Coaches Notes: Collaboration is the new competition. Have an abundance mentality and I promise you it will pay off big time. All of these top leaders are great collaborators. I see it at our six and seven figure masterminds. The very top leaders in this industry come together at my masterminds and share openly and authentically about their businesses. All of these leaders have watched training from their companies as well as outside their companies. Successful leaders have such thirst for learning that they figure out how to become better and take their business to the next level. They are truly committed.

Take Action Fast

Action and effort create results. The faster you take action, the sooner you will have success. You can go as fast or as slow as you want, but as the saying goes, "success loves speed." You don`t have to know everything, but you do have to take action. Be ignorance on fire, not knowledge on ice. Learn and EARN together. Ask questions, make mistakes (that is part of the process). I have seen success fast in multiple companies simply because I RAN, hard and fast. I didn`t have all the details, BUT I was EXCITED and got to work.

Today is a new day. Whether you have been in your company a month or a year, you have the ability to start over and launch again. GET EXCITED!! Excitement beats experience hands down. In reality we should ALWAYS be launching our businesses. I challenge you, take the RIGHT action (not sitting watching training videos all day and fake working, but actually doing IPA`s daily) and KNOW YOUR NUMBERS. You will eventually find the success you are looking for if you remain open to coaching, stay consistent and dream big. When you get stuck or feel frustrated, remember why you started. I promise, if you tap into your why, you will cross oceans to make your dreams a reality.

Author: Aron Parker

- Placed third at the National Speed Skating championship at fifteen years old.

- Personally enrolled hundreds of people with current business.

- Earned over one MILLION in commissions with current business in two years.

- Winner of several top awards within his company

- Team of over 5,000 members

- In network marketing for over years

*Tough times never last
but tough people do.
If it is to be... it's up to me!*

I first started in business as the rule breaker. You aren`t supposed to join until you are eighteen, but I started at seventeen... I was ready for entrepreneurship! Even at that age I could see the potential for greatness in this industry, and I wanted in! I had the vision, but no clue what I was doing, and so right after high school I joined The Marines. I was actually going to join the AirForce, but after the Marine recruiter sat down with me, looked into my eyes and told me I could be the BEST... I was ALL-IN! The biggest thing I learned from being a Marine is that we have much more inside of us than we think... they will push you to the LIMIT and then past it knowing you can!

I joined several companies over the years, and from each company I learned something and grew in my experience. By the time I was married with two young kids, I had made some money, but not enough to sustain us with network marketing only. I found myself working a job I really did not like in Elkhart, IN (where my wife is from) at a RV trailer factory and working my network marketing business on my lunch breaks and after my kids went to bed. It was a real grind and something had to change because we were broke! I knew we could break FREE! And finally, in 2012. we did, going full time in Network Marketing making six figures!

Daily Methods

People always want the one secret to success, and I always tell them that it isn`t a secret. It is a SIMPLE daily method of operation done consistently. I spent my time making connections with NEW people and following up every single day. Success didn`t happen quickly... But the work finally paid off. It felt like one day everything just clicked into place. I went from some side money in network marketing to six figures. I was able to quit my job and go full time... most people simply are not willing to put in the work daily.

Here`s the crazy thing, just as quickly as it came into our lives, it left our lives. The company we built up to six figures started to lose all momentum, and so did our paycheck. Then one day it was gone... out of business! We weren`t prepared for that. We struggled to find something else and it failed... several times! We had no money, and our savings were gone. None of our bills were paid. We couldn`t even pay rent, and our bank account was in the negative. I am an eternal optimist, and I told my wife everything would be ok, but she told me she may have to take our kids and go back to her family... that`s how bad it got.

As a man who wants to provide for his family, that was a huge wake up call. I couldn`t blame companies or my team. I had to take extreme ownership of the situation and tell myself that I had put us there. Many people are going through some hard times right now. I want you to really look closely at what is going on and ask yourself serious questions... "Can I do more?"

Extreme ownership of my own dire situation and realizing I was the one that did that, was hard, but it also motivated me. I had nothing and no one to blame but myself. I was going to find something. I knew that it had to be the one.

So how do you start with your first company, or in my case, start over? You have to go back to the daily actions. What you do in your DMO is the most important thing. I had to launch my business to save my family. The very first month with the company I did $10k and since have made a million dollars!

My DMO at the beginning was basically stop everything in my life. There was no balance or structure or wondering what I would do next. It was all about prospecting from the moment I got up. It was 12, 14, 16 hours a day. It was like that for ninety days nonstop. That burst of energy and action with no structure blew my business up. It came down to one question, "Is what I am doing right now going to produce a result?" That's it.... That's the SECRET! I didn't organize my desk. I didn't spend time thinking about anything else. I had to be ALL-IN! Is what I am doing right now going to produce a result? If the answer is no, I'm not doing it. Your upline can help you figure out what your DMO should look like, but you can start by asking yourself the question I asked myself every single day.

Coaches Notes: I love that Aron takes 100 percent responsibility. One of my first conversations with him was after he had become a top earner. He immediately told me about his failures, which were learning lessons. He immediately talked about weaknesses he was working on. He has overcome so much because of his ability to focus. This ability to focus comes from his DMO. Each person will have a different DMO, but you must have one. You see, we are used to being told what to do by our parents, teachers and bosses.

Now you get to do what you want when you want. Unfortunately most network marketers procrastinate and are massively unproductive. A DMO protects you from being inefficient. It gives you focus to build your dreams quicker. Decide what are the things you commit to everyday to build your business. Hint ... the #1 income producing activity is talking to new people about your business or products.

How To Get Started

As a team leader of thousands of people, I know that everyone is at a different place. As you think about yourself or your first handful of recruits, ask these questions. Questions help you to see where they are at and what their goals are.

- What is your experience with network marketing?

- What are your expectations? What are you expecting with this business?

- How much money do you need to make?

- Why do you need to make that type of money?"

Identify what they want and SHOW them how to get there. It is a daily journey to help them build. It involves posting on social media and talking to people daily. You are setting people up to know about the journey and process of this business. You have to let people know what to expect!

Occasionally, people won`t be clear about what their true motivation is. Maybe they don`t know it, or they don`t want to say. But understand that their motivation will come up again and again in your business. When you first start out, I want you to really think about what motivates you. Because when the business gets tough, it`s your motivation that keeps you going.

I do promos in our groups with prizes and people will tell me they are so excited. But when it comes right down to it, most people still don`t do the work. So what is going to motivate them? Everyone is different.

Get crystal clear about what is going to motivate you. If you don`t have that, you`re done! You aren`t going to make it. This is tough. It`s not easy. When it gets tough, what is motivating you to move forward? You have to have baby steps and baby wins to help people have success. It`s not easy, but it`s WORTH IT!

Prospect Everywhere

The actual work of your DMO involves prospecting and talking to people. We do the basics. We need to get people that you know to look at the business.

The very best thing I have always done in my business is building relationships for the past eight years. I reached out to everyone with massive prospecting and massive actions. I have been completely obsessed with building the life I want.

There is a HUGE mistake I see people make when they first start out. They don't act proud of starting a business! You have to take ownership of what you are doing, and be proud of what you are doing. Be proud of starting a business, be proud about your product, and let other people know what you are up to.

You don't have to shove it down their throat, but you have to at least reach out and tell them what you are doing. Make it easy. Reach out and tell them what you are doing and say something like, "I would love to get your opinion." or "I would love for you to try it out so that I can get some testimonials." You could even ask, "Would anyone you know want to make an extra thousand dollars a month working from home?" Start with who you know and go through your warm market.

Coaches Notes: Have lives in your company been changed because of network marketing?

Have lives in the network marketing industry been changed because they joined this industry?

In one study it said that 85% of people hate their jobs. This isn`t to rip on jobs because some love them and they are necessary. This is to give you perspective that people are looking for what you have. Open your mouth! Look for opportunities to have people check out your business and products. You are not selling them on joining. You are selling them on taking a look. You got this!

Your Million Dollar Network

Part of my specialty is Facebook. I have built my entire business without spending any money on marketing. I have built it through Facebook and grew my network. Can you imagine building a million dollar business and not spending a dime on marketing? I am able to do that because of my network. I call it my "million-dollar network". Because what I have built, the relationships I have authentically created, and the business has generated is what have helped me build my success.

Anyone can have a million-dollar network, and that includes you. I want to teach you how to start growing your very own million dollar network. On Facebook, I do two things. I use attraction marketing, which you can read more about in this book. People may think that it is easy for me to do it online because of my network and it is easier now. But I have been in the place that many of you are. I have such an amazing network because of what I had done in the past on Facebook before having any success. Remember... every PRO was once an AMATEUR.

I`m always making new friends. Before, I would do my posts, and get crickets on it. Not a lot of comments or likes. I had to shift my perspective and make it about other people. I started going out and liking and commenting on other people`s posts. I was seeking out people that I wanted to work with and making sure we started to have connections.

I started to have people follow me and start to engage on my posts because I was doing that on their profiles and feeds. Once that started happening, I would make curiosity posts, "I just made $100! Woohoo!

Who wants to learn how to do it?" People started to engage. That small success of $100 is more than most people expect This is another mistake people make. They hold off on telling people what they are doing until they make it big. It doesn`t have to be big. Post any success, even small and see how people respond. But, it can`t just stop there. You have to do the real work, which is messaging prospects back and forth daily.

Once people have liked or commented on your post, take it into messenger. Start a conversation and ask them questions. This is the perfect way to start to talk about what you have going on and how you can help them.

When I first started doing this I was still working a full time job. I would get up at 5:00am while my family was still sleeping and hit my prospecting online. I would be in messenger prospecting on my lunch break while all the other guys were sitting around chilling. Every night I would be prospecting until midnight.... getting four to five hours of sleep because I was MOTIVATED to change my life! How motivated are you daily?

It goes back to the question of... "Is what I am doing right now getting me results?" I would message at least twenty people a day. I was aggressively making new friends. People ask me how I would find all of these people. Easy! I was aggressively looking for them.

From there, just make it fun. I am just making friends and connecting and we are talking about their business and how it is going. In the conversation I would bring up what I was doing and ask for their feedback or opinion.

It was just an exchange in conversation. I was building my network, making new friends, having great conversations. Sometimes, I will even pitch in our initial conversation because people are busy and will appreciate you getting to the point. Now, when I post, many more people will engage. They see I am having success and they want in on the action. They qualify themselves to come to my team... everyone wants to be on a WINNING team!

The key to this is that it has to become a way of life. It has to become every day. It is the compound effect. Are you willing to put in the work daily? It doesn't happen overnight. It sometimes takes a while, but many people are watching you and will join when the time is right for them..... Maybe three weeks, three months or even three years later!

Find people to be friends with. Go into groups that you have things in common with and reach out. Find the people that you are interested in. Ask questions and build relationships. Do that ten times a day. Build ten new relationships a day. If you are consistent with it, you are going to enroll people in your business. Be PASSIONATE, Be EXCITED, and you will have success.

It Is Bigger Than You

I told you about how I almost lost the most precious thing to me; my family. This business is incredible, and there is huge potential to make money, become a leader, and even to be well known in the industry. But this business isn`t really about you. It is so much bigger.

I get that you may need to make money right now, but if you want staying capacity in this industry, you have to find a reason bigger than you.

Mine was the reality of losing my family and being broke! Most of us will work harder for someone else. For me, it was my wife and kids. Before, when I wasn`t having success in this business, I was doing it for myself. It wasn`t hitting and working because it was all about me. When I finally saw my wife and kids and saw how much they needed me, I became Superman in network marketing and did whatever it took to make it work.

We are doing well now for ourselves, and now that bigger reason has expanded out from my wife and kids. I want to be able to help my mom so she doesn`t have to worry about money and her future. I want to help my team have success just like we have.

There are things in our lives that are bigger than us. It could be something like a charity. We are very passionate about helping Operation Underground Railroad. We have two little girls and to see what is happening to children all over the world was heartbreaking. We wanted to be part of the organization and the people that dedicate their lives to stopping these horrendous crimes against children. Now I am building my business not just for my wife and kids. Not just for my mom, not just for my team, but to save little kids. Now it becomes bigger. Now every time I get to run my business, I have a bigger cause that is relying on me to show up and grow. You have to figure out, even the brand new person, what is the thing that is bigger than you. When you figure that out and see the business as the vehicle to get you there, it is magic.

Many people say it`s their "WHY".... it has to make you cry.

I believe we need to find our "HAVE TO".

Why do you HAVE TO create success with your business?

Figure out what that is, and you will become UNSTOPPABLE!

Coaches Notes: The one commonality you will find with all of these leaders is that they created a strong enough why. They created a strong enough vision to get through the hard times. It isn`t that they didn`t have hard times. Every single leader has had doubts. It is that these leaders pushed through. This industry is incredible. There are so many events, mastermind retreats and access to great content that will help you have success but none of that matters if you don`t get clear on WHY you are doing this business. Figure that out and everything else will fall into place.

Author: Essie Prigge

- Over fifty million dollars in sales in three years

- Nine thousand active on the team

- Rank number eleven on national team

- Gemstone National Executive Director

- Presidential Circle Team Member

- Qualified for every incentive trip, price, etc

"First think, second dream, third believe, and finally, dare."

-Walt Disney

Top Income Earner

I found network marketing when my child got diagnosed with cancer. I realized at that time that my 9-5 job had made me very unavailable for him when he had gotten sick. I made a promise to myself that I wouldn't stay at a job that didn't support me supporting my family. It's difficult as parents, as a mom that I was having to choose between being there for my child and working my job. I didn't want to sacrifice the things that were most important to me for a paycheck. When I found network marketing I knew it was going to be a blessing for us because it fit all of my criteria of being able to work from home on my own terms and still be there for my family.

I learned really quickly how to become successful in this business. The best part was that it was simple. Now let me stop right here because I was to say that just because it is simple, doesn't mean it is easy. It is important for everyone to know that the skills to be successful are simple, but not easy. This is a JOB and it takes work. The principles are simple, the execution isn't always easy. I want to share with you the simple principles that I I have built a successful business using, all while being able to be there for my family.

Coaches Notes: I was able to hear Essie's story and get to know her at one of my "Leader of Leaders" masterminds. She blew me away with how well her systems are in place. The last line from the above paragraph is so important to understand. "The principles are simple, the execution isn't always easy." Too many people confuse simple for easy. Of course, this business isn't easy. If it were easy everyone would do it. Leonardo Davinci said it best, "Simplicity is the ultimate sophistication." This next chapter will give you insights on how to master simple and keep the main focus ... the main focus.

Simple principle #1 Be authentic. People can tell when you aren`t being yourself and you are trying to fit a mold. It comes off as fake, and people don`t want to do business or buy from someone that is fake. Not everyone is going to like what you stand for and what you have to say, and that is ok. You have to learn to be true to who you are because it attracts the right people. The right people are your people! Business is better when you are authentic and you are standing true to what you believe in and showing what makes you tick. Standing for who I was made a huge difference.

From day one, I told myself I wouldn`t change who I was. I was going to go after what I wanted and work hard, but I was going to stick to my ethics and morals. I have been able to do that and it makes a difference. Always be authentic and real with people. Be transparent with people. They appreciate and respect that.

Simple principle #2 Always be a student of your business. Doesn`t matter what business it is. If it`s network marketing or something else. We can always learn and grow more. Always be a student of the business because you can learn from every single opportunity. Be open to starting from square one. Find a mentor that you can align with. Ask questions, do your homework, push yourself out of your comfort zone.

You need to always be looking for ways to improve and be open to learn from other people and other places. When I was new, I had to put my pride aside and do the work to learn something new. It didn`t matter that I had 20 years of corporate experience. I needed to learn about this business.

I needed to educate myself about this industry. I didn`t know, and I had to start from scratch and do the work. Educate yourself and learn from the best. Be open to learn.

I went into network marketing open and soaking up the information from the right people. It is important to know who you are learning from. Align with people that inspire you that will take you under their wing and mentor you.

Simple principle #3 Don't just recruit to recruit. Be honest with the people you are recruiting. Don't just take anyone. Sometimes people in network marketing will not be honest with a prospective recruit or they try and sugarcoat what this business really looks like. It is not as simple as posting on social media and people come flocking to you.

It is important to be intentional and be honest with people and tell them about the hard work it takes. If they are an introvert and not willing to do the work, it probably isn't a match for you and them. I use this as an example because people think it just takes numbers. It is so much more than the numbers. People that you are talking to have to be willing to do the work.

Don't just get your numbers; recruit with intention. They can interview you, but you should also be interviewing them. Make sure they are willing to do the work. Sometimes we just get excited about someone saying yes, but it is about more than the yes. It is finding the people that are looking for the same thing you are looking for. It is more than getting a warm body on the team. Make sure you are a match with someone.

You don't want to get into a business relationship and have them not realize what they got themselves into. Make sure it is a good fit for both of you! Think of it as an interview for a job. Interview and ask the open-ended questions that help you get to know them so you can be the best leader for them. Sometimes people don't know what they are saying yes to. Dive in and talk about the good, the bad, and the ugly with people so that you can really show them what it takes to make this business work and take the next step.

Coaches Notes: This tip from Essie will save you so much time! We get it. When you begin in this business or even if you are just struggling you typically are just happy if anyone signs up. Sometimes we get so desperate that we tell white lies. We don`t directly lie but we don`t give the full truth on what this business really takes. This isn`t to say you should start out by trying to scare your newest prospect but more that you should do a better job of casting a simple vision. This simple vision that you are going to give is going to be focused on their goals. If one has a goal to make $300 a month then don`t sugarcoat the path to get there. Obviously the higher the goals the more it will take to achieve those goals. The main principle is to discover how to recruit with the right intention. This will attract better-qualified prospects, create a better culture and improve retention dramatically.

Simple principle #4 Time is precious. We all have the same 24 hours in a day. Time freedom and working on our own is one of the most amazing perks about this business. You have to be up front and do the work as you recruit for your future. You don`t want to waste your time because YOU haven`t been crystal clear about what is expected of people up front.

We all value our time. Alot of us join this industry because it allows us freedom of time. Use it on the right people. Invest it on the right people up front. It is important to set the expectations instead of just getting the big numbers in the door. You might not think it will take up your time, but it. The time upfront will save you time on the back end. Know what you are looking for and don`t just lead blindly.

Simple principle #5 Ask the questions. You may not want to ask the questions, but you need to. Be honest and let them know if it isn`t the opportunity for them. When you`re building your team and looking for the future. Have they done their research? What are they looking for from this business? What are they willing to commit to be successful?

I ask people where they see themselves in six months and where they see themselves in a year. I ask them what they know about our company. It helps to get a feel for where they are at and what they have in mind. You want professionals as your leaders. You want them to be the caliber to lead. Sometimes it`s hard for people to ask the questions, but be open and honest and you may need to give them some tough love and tell them what it really takes to make this business work.

It works because it is a crystal clear guide and people know what they are getting into. No one wants to get hired for a job and then not know what they got themselves into. You want to set your company or new employee up for success. It`s the same with network marketing. They know what you are looking for and they know your expectations. You will also want to know their expectations of you and the industry.

Simple principle #6 This is a business. It needs to be treated like one. Be crystal clear to yourself and others that you are running a business. This is an opportunity to build a business. You have to stress that this is business. You must invest the time and do the work.

I love the example of Lugi, who`s lifelong dream was to open a pizza place. He saves every penny he has and takes his entire life savings to open up his new business. He isn`t going to just sit behind the counter and wait for people to come. He has to get out and promote his business, he has to invest into his business, he has to do the work. He isn`t going to be shy and not tell his friends and family about the pizza shop! He is going to be out there telling everyone about this new business he has opened. Be like Lugi and let people know that you have opened a business and do the work!!

Network marketing isn`t going to take your life savings, but it is going to take work. You have to put the time in. You have to be a student of the business.

The newest members need strong leaders. Recruit for your future. Ask the questions. Ask them what they see in the business opportunity. Know what they are looking for and figure out how to identify it. Day one into this business and you need to be intentional about your recruiting. You want someone that wants to build for their future. When you are interviewing and recruiting you want to be up front. Be open and transparent about what it takes to be successful in this business.

Most people are unrealistic with what it takes to do this business. They see people at the top and they think they got there because they have a big following. This business is only as good as last month`s sales. You have to be constantly pouring into your team. You have to be constantly growing. You have to be constantly recruiting. Most people don`t see the behind the scenes and what it takes to have success.

Simple principle #7 A strategy that helps recruit for your future online is cultivating relationships. In my last business I kept in contact with people that I worked with. I share what I am doing now and ask them if they know anyone that is wanting a business opportunity for entrepreneurs.

There was a woman that I worked with previously. I could see her talent and knew that she would be amazing at this business. I reached out to her and told her this would be awesome for her because of the talent that she had. I let her know about that opportunity, but I also interviewed her and let her know what would be expected.

Fast forward to several years later and she is now one of the best leaders on my team. I wanted to know if she had what it would take and if she was committed. It did take her some time, but she always says that she was grateful that I was a talent picker and presented the business opportunity to her. I was willing to tell her what I was looking for and I listened to what she needed in a business opportunity.

An important thing in this industry is to be a talent picker. We all have seen people that have a certain talent. Who is on your list Dream Team list... Who do you see that has the talent to be successful in this business, don`t be afraid to tap those people on the shoulder and tell them that you think their talents align with what you are looking for to build your team. Always be on the lookout for talent. Don`t hesitate to go out and be a talent picker.

Simple principle #8 Don't let fear hold you back. Fear of rejection holds so many people back. You have to be transparent and ask people in the beginning how they handle fear. What they do with obstacles or rejection. You will be surprised what people say.

Overcoming fear held me back. I was afraid to fail. I didn`t want to be the spammy person and I was so afraid of what people would think of me and my business. But when I changed my mindset from worrying what people thought to following my dreams...What I wanted financial freedom, being the best present mom to my kids, my dreams always outweighed my fear. People get paralyzed by fear and it holds them back. When recruiting and buying your dream team, ask them- what their biggest fear is and be honest about what it takes to overcome that fear.

Simple principle #9 Allow the industry to change you. I am a completely different person because of this business. It has helped me elevate my life. It has helped me create confidence and know that I can do anything I put my mind to. Now with a team of almost 9000 I know I can do the hard things and overcome my fears. I can dream more than I ever thought and go after it even when I am scared. I have overcome fear in network marketing and I can overcome fear anywhere. You can dream big and you can achieve big.

Go hard. Dream big. I like to tell my team, Dream big, Dream bigger, Dream biggest. I did my homework and joined someone that is so successful. When I joined I asked how many people she had on her team and they told me 8000. I couldn`t even imagine having that huge of a team. My big goal was 100 people on my team. My bigger goal was 1000. My biggest scariest goal was 8000. I just accomplished that, and it still gives me chills. It is mind blowing to me that I have achieved that in three years. Be a student of the business always. Take the good, take the bad, and learn from it.

I was a naysayer of network marketing. I wasn`t somebody who saw myself doing this. Life had other plans for me. When my son got sick, I had to pivot and do something different. This business showed me that you can really do whatever you want to do. Learn, invest, ask the questions, trial and error, the people that are at the top have failed too. That makes us human. Everyday isn`t perfect but you have to look at the end goal and be willing to commit and do the work. Invest in yourself. I am forever grateful for this industry. Don`t say it`s easy, it is a lot of work. But it can be simple. And have FUN!!! This business can change your life!!

Coaches Notes: These 9 steps give you the map for success in your business. As Essie mentioned they are simple but they take time to execute. I remember hearing years ago Tony Robbins give his definition of happiness. PROGRESS. That`s it. When you are progressing you are happy. If you want to have success focus on progress, not perfection. Focus on executing these simple steps. One way to truly execute these steps is to do a weekly assessment. Assess yourself every week on how you are doing with the 9 steps. Assess yourself on what you did well and what you can do better. Then keep PROGRESSING! Those small daily steps over the course of a year will add up to a whole lot of PROGRESS. Simple progress will lead to massive success.

Authors: Britt And Matt Riddell

MATT

- Began as a customer for 2 years.

- Recruited 38 people in his first 90 days.

- Went full- time in 2012 and has been with one company for 15 years.

- First Gen Y Diamond in company history.

- Company advisory board member.

- Eleven-time annual conference and leadership keynote speaker.

- Driven by helping people step up and live their best life.

BRITT

- Has been with her company for 5 years, full-time for 3.

- One of the youngest 6 figure Elites in company history.

- Company product innovation advisory board member.

- Annual conference and industry event speaker.

- Multiple incentive trip winner.

- Fiercely passionate about helping people discover network marketing

"It's totally possible for you to design and live an extraordinary life"

On How We Got Started

MATT & BRITT

When we both reflect back, it's almost like we didn't choose network marketing - it chose us. Neither of us were specifically looking for a network marketing business, but we were definitely looking for what it offers - a better way to do life. We each wanted more options, more freedom and exciting income potential.

MATT

I totally believe that for anyone with an entrepreneurial spirit, network marketing is the ultimate business vehicle. Why? One word. Leverage. Very few employees actually appreciate how powerful this concept is. What's leverage? Put simply, it's the power of people. What sets our industry apart from everything else is that you, as a business owner, can recruit other business owners - and if you're a leader, you can grow an amazing organization. As a young entrepreneur, I had my first business by the age of 22, and after two years of traditional hiring and firing, I just knew there had to be a better way. Hence, the reason I was so drawn to investigating what network marketing had to offer. It was a combination of frustration and inspiration. Frustrated at trying to get ahead in small business, and inspired by people I was meeting who were literally living the dream through network marketing. I didn't say yes right away because I had other commitments, but when the time was right and I made my decision, it was like a switch got flicked. Within the first four years I broke every record in the company history and became the youngest diamond ever. There's a lesson there - keep in touch with people. Imagine if my sponsor had given up because I said no at the start. Keep a vision and see what's possible for people - that's real leadership.

BRITT

I bleed network marketing. I was born into the industry and when I was growing up, it was normal to talk about goals and dreams and going after what you wanted in life. Mum and dad probably didn`t realize that by saying yes to network marketing just how impactful their decision would really be for me. I was watching their every move and example. Children are so perceptive and take on everything you do and say. I believe leadership starts at home, and I encourage anyone who is involved in this industry to get your kids involved, too. I adopted their work ethic just because they were leading by example. My parents taught me that I really could be or do anything I want in life. They taught me to dream and they gave me a taste of what the industry promise is all about. Every night when mum and dad would tuck me into bed, they would ask me the same question, and they would answer it in the same way. They would ask me, "Britt what do you want to do or be when you grow up?"

I had no clue I was five years old. But they would tell me, "Britt, you can be anything you want to be, and you can do anything you want to do if you put your heart to it". That affirmation stuck. That little girl grew up believing just that. This is the magic part of this industry that I would like to highlight! Most people are walking around out there not realizing their full potential, because somebody didn`t give them permission to dream BIG or tell them that they actually can achieve it or give them a game plan on how to do that. Talk to your kids about dreams, goals, and fill those little dear hearts up with endless possibilities. It really does start here first. You are changing the world through your children, too. This is where your legacy begins.

So naturally, by having entrepreneurial parents and knowing that other options existed, I didn`t want to work the 45 year plan, I didn`t want to be told what I was worth (per hour) and I didn`t want to be ruled by an alarm clock. I wanted a lifestyle that I could fall in love with, and I knew this industry was real!

When I was old enough I "dabbled" in a few different companies, trying to figure it out and find my feet. I actually decided that network marketing wasn`t for me at that time and I may review it later. Looking back now with more experienced eyes, old school tactics didn`t work and neither did secret squirrel business. There was no real method for duplication with a proven system for anyone to win at, no matter what their skill level, and I really didn`t have the patience as a generation Y to figure that all out. I probably wasn`t even ready for that type of leadership or responsibility yet, I had to grow, and everything is always timing. Despite my enthusiasm and belief in the industry, I was slightly disheartened at my experience, but I knew I could recreate that and there was an answer somewhere, but I just parked network marketing on the side for a moment. It wasn`t until my dearest girlfriend Hannah, who is just a raving fan customer (not a business builder!), invited me along to a wine and cheese overview night where I met my now husband Matthew! Hannah who was advocating passionately about products she had discovered really got my interest. I thought it was fascinating that a customer was promoting a business event, and I thought "wow, they must have nailed customer culture," and this concept had my attention. I didn`t dive in straight away, I wanted to make sure this was the "one." In fact, Matt had outstanding follow up, and kept inviting me to the next thing - both two important principles with network marketing that everyone should implement ASAP in their business. Together we now have a global multi-million-dollar business, and I wouldn`t change it for anything. I absolutely love what I do, and I love the fact that I met Matt through networking!

On What Works

MATT + BRITT

We have seen so many patterns emerge of what works, and what doesn`t work in network marketing. One of the biggest gaps we see in network marketing is that people sign others up and don`t take them on the growth journey.

They just sign them up and say, "Off you go." You must be invested in the development of your newest people. This isn`t a business that is a "one and done". You have to create systems that support the development of others. We have set up a system that tells them exactly what the next step is. Once they accomplish that, they move onto the next step. It is simple. Otherwise, people don`t know what to do.

> **Coaches Notes:** Not only do Matt and Britt have amazing Aussie accents but they are incredible leaders that give a very unique perspective. Each one of them spoke at an event I hosted in Australia. I was impressed with their ability to break things down and simplify complex ideas. They understand the value of systems to create a long lasting business. Part of creating great systems is focusing on the development of your team. This section will be a next level type section to give you a vision of what you want and need in order to take your business to the highest ranks.

MATT

You will come across laser focused entrepreneurs who just join and crush it, but lots of people take time. For example, when I first got started, you could buy a business in a bag for about $400. It had a system handbook, a bunch of books, CD`s and a few DVD`s, and was literally the best $400 I ever invested. I sponsored 38 people in 90 days and the rest is history. That said, it`s important to remember that a majority of people who join us don`t have business experience, so making sure that the tools and frameworks exist so that anyone can learn at their own pace and grow into leadership is critical. Spend your time working with leaders, but be there for everyone and have the support systems in place so everyone can win.

BRITT

It`s true! People need to be guided. They are diving into something that is new and with new comes fears and limiting beliefs. These feelings are only natural and with a duplicatable system with simple steps partnered with action, coachability and a support team your newest person will be well on their way to personal growth and business growth!

If you are teaching someone to drive a car, you don`t tell them everything at once. You teach them what to do, one thing at a time and you show them. People learn by doing, with someone in the copilot seat. Just like driving. The temptation is to take over and do it for them, but they will never learn.

The best thing is let them do it averagely and be there with them encouraging and directing. With practice, they will get better and better, courage will turn into competence and competence will turn into confidence. Watching people grow is the best part of what we do.

With access to endless information, there are so many different things available. You have so many "industry experts" coaching in this space, particularly with social media and for someone new, it can be very overwhelming. Even people who want to be big influencers using social media have to start with a simple first step process so that it can be duplicated down the line. I have a love/ hate relationship with social media as I would rather have leaders than followers as an influencer. What you do must always be duplicatable and simple for the newest person to implement and get results.

On Systems

MATT

Bruce Lee said, "I don`t fear a man that has done 10,000 kicks once, I fear the man that has done one kick 10,000 times." That is getting in and learning the skills. Think about someone going to University. What happens if you go two of the three years. You don`t get your degree. Same thing here. A typical MBA takes eight years. You can earn an MBA in this business as well. If you invested your time, energy, and growth into this business for eight years, and do it, you don`t leave with a piece of paper - you come out with a Massive Bank Account.

Now, at the time of this book we are at a crossroads of new meets old, offline meets online, and there is a lot of confusion as to 'what works` and following systems. Especially for people like me! If you`re over 35 and you`ve been in network marketing for more than a decade, you`ll know *exactly* what I mean.

Here`s my take on it. The one thing that doesn`t change is the fact that we are a relationship business. Period. The forms of connection and communication we use have evolved, and as leaders we need to make sure our systems are constantly evolving to meet the changing way people communicate with each other.

BRITT

We created a Facebook group that has units so everyone can train on how to do the business. Right from the start, we are aiming to get new recruits into momentum. We are launching people, not joining people. We give them exact directions.

Give people the exact next step; just like we mentioned before. We blend the traditional principles with what`s relevant now. We have them do a curiosity post (with ideas already mapped out for them) on social media as it`s an easy way to share an experience and it`s an indirect way to see who is looking for what you have got. We have them make a 10 best and 10 easiest list.

Who are your ten best people that you would like to recruit into your team?

Who are the ten easiest people to recruit to your team?

Helping them reach out and start conversations and invite is really important. Connection equals relationships and relationships equal business. We help and guide them through that. We also leverage the three-way messenger chat and help them through this. This is new, and you may need to hold their hand and guide them. In the beginning I teach them to be a really good connector while they have their training wheels on. That way, they can be guided while they are creating their new business muscle.

For as far as training goes, create a system, follow it, and make it easy to use. Maybe your upline or sponsor has something already in place. Don`t reinvent it. Get into the system and use it! You have to have it so easy that someone that is ready to go can go through your training on a weekend. Because they will do it. Winners are going to win. You need to have room for your rockstar, or they will find someone else to win with.

MATT

Thanks to social media, no leader, no matter how successful you have been in the past, can rest on yesterday`s achievements. The world is so much more transparent and you need to constantly keep learning and stay in the field practicing to remain relevant. Lucky for us, this is the most fun and rewarding profession there is, especially if it`s done in an authentic, natural way.

BRITT

For us, we literally do business as we do life, and we totally love it. It`s all about changing people`s lives.

Coaches Notes: When people join your business, they aren`t just joining the business. They are joining YOU. They are joining a team. They are joining a system. Why do so many people buy franchises? They want a system. This gives them direction. People want a plan. People want some sort of security. People want proof of a system. Matt and Britt get this so well. They understand the value of following a simple system. If your team has one, then follow it. If your team doesn`t have one and you are overwhelmed, then start small and follow the guidelines from this section.

Become System Dependent Not Leader Dependent

MATT

Confession. My business was very "Matt dependent" for a long time. You can figure out if your business is only about you if you are getting all of your volume from your first four levels. It is difficult to take it lower than that if the business is built on you. When your business becomes system dependent, it will build like crazy. It literally explodes. For lots of people - me included - this is the shift that will take you from struggle to success, from frustration to inspiration. It`s the true game changer for your business.

BRITT

We are super system driven, and obsessed by making it fun, simple, easy, and duplicatable. And if you do it right, it`s magical. People can join your business, upskill themselves, and be winning super quick.

Create A Raving Fan Culture

MATT + BRITT

One of the most valuable things we do is create our own team culture and customer culture. We love our company. We love the culture, but it can change. Companies change all the time, and we really have to invest in what we can control. We are fully in control of our team culture and customer culture.

We drive the team culture. We create a super strong product culture, and we don`t lose when we focus on the product. The customer culture is huge. You have to be passionate and live and breathe what you are doing. It is hard to do something if you aren`t passionate about what you are doing. Think for yourself about how you are going to create a customer and team culture from the beginning. It doesn`t have to be elaborate. Just think about how you will treat your customers. Think about what type of team you want to have and cultivate. It can be easy with simple things done consistently. Our philosophy is simple - aim to create raving fans. Not only do they become your most dedicated, loyal, loud customers, they`ll often be your best recruits!

On Commitment

MATT

Be before you are and you will become. If you want to have a huge team, then act like it today. Be consistent and act the part. I can only give what I know works. When I started my personal training studio in 2004, I remember sitting there with a document for a $55k loan. I told myself, "If I sign this, I am all in." There was no backing out. I signed the loan docs and got to work. I treated this business exactly the same from the first day. I signed that application form, and got to work.

Make the decision to do network marketing and stick with it for a minimum of five years. If you don`t have the skills it doesn`t matter, you have time to learn. It doesn`t matter what other people are doing, start where you are and commit to being all in for five years. Make a decision and show up for five years, and show up like you have $55k on the line.

BRITT

It is a decision to be a leader. It`s not something that is given, it`s taken. You are a part of something bigger than you when you decide to lead. Leading is showing up and being an example for others. You don`t need to have a team (yet) to lead. It`s about implementing leadership principles as soon as you get started. Commitment and leadership go hand in hand in my opinion. Whatever you decide to do with your life, you have to be all in. You have to have a decided heart. You have to not just do the things, but decide in your heart that you are all in. Energy is everything, and your heart is at the hub of it. I love to see people grow like our introverts in our team because they have made a commitment to their future self. What people transform into is so gratifying, and most people surprise themselves as they level up, kick goals, grow, contribute and conquer! Just remember, it all starts with commitment. There have been plenty of occasions where the team has been committed to a particular outcome (maybe a new rank title as an example) and sometimes the outcome can feel as though it is not in reach but because we are committed to making things happen, we double down as a team with activity and things can move very fast with intention. Leadership is two things. Sacrifice and service. As soon as you decide to sacrifice, to go above and beyond and serve others, you are a leader.

On What Is Working Right Now

MATT

Be willing to see what is relevant now and adjust to it. There was a fixed system for twenty years. What happened was the internet came and changed everything, especially with social media. It comes to getting products in people`s hands. Doesn`t matter how you do it.

BRITT

It totally comes down to conversations. You can create content on social media all day long, but it really is how willing you are to have conversations - whether it be online or offline. Connect, invite, and offer.

Content might be king, but conversation is queen. By getting to know someone, you really can discover how best you can serve them. How can you change that person`s life through what this industry has to offer? Think about walking into a pub and sitting next to someone on a stool. You can say all of your amazing content and it would be weird. They would probably move, or worse! You have to start a conversation. People don`t care about your content unless they see that you are interested in them. Add value! Start a conversation. Start a simple conversation. Care. Be interested in others while everyone else is focused on being interesting! It gives you a tremendous advantage. Frazer Brooks uses LORD (location, occupation, recreation, and dreams and desires). Do this, and you will know that person better than half of their friends - and as we know, people do business with people they know, like and trust.

The Power Of Events

MATT + BRITT

For us, events have been the key to business growth. 100 percent. Leaders are born at events. Decisions are made at events. Lives are changed at events. From a recruiting prospective, we build our business from event to event.

MATT

I got recruited because my sponsors invited me to an event. In fact, I went to four of them before I made a decision! The event does the work for you, you just have to invite people.

It also gives our team an actionable step to take for the week. We tell them, their job is to invite people to this one event for the week.

Here are the magic words for the invite, "Hey listen, there is an event on such and such a date and I thought you might want to know about it because...." And then you fill in the blanks because you know that person. I never randomly invite someone to an event until I have a relationship and know how I can serve them.

BRITT

It is always evolving. Our mentors always taught us, always have events! It is key. In fact, that is how I was introduced by my dear friend Hannah. It doesn`t matter if it is in person or online. As we said, leaders are born at events. Want more leaders? Have more events. We do Monday night training. 90 percent of our team is on these calls because we keep it short and sweet, usually 45 minutes. We always give them the action item for the week, as well.

I think the biggest thing that holds people back in network marketing is their hesitation with the unknown. They are doing something they have never done and going someplace they have never been. So naturally your brain tries to protect you and tell you it is scary. It is actually nature taking over here. It`s instinct and has been happening for millions of years to protect our species from danger. You must overcome that. Action cures fear.

The Magic Belief - It's Not About You

It's all about making a difference. We have shared some of our top ways to keep your business thriving and not making it all about you. This business is about people. The more you can go out and help people succeed, the more your business thrives. We always say that your bonus each month shows how many people you helped that month. Watch your wealth grow as you help people grow. Make it simple on yourself by creating systems that work for you, and always be willing to grow with the team culture leading the way.

Coaches Notes: As mentioned by Britt and Matt social media is incredible but it means nothing if you aren't having those daily conversations. I cannot stress this enough. There is no secret strategy that teaches you to avoid having those daily conversations. You still need to have those and focus on them daily. That is why The Network Marketing strategy planner/tracker is so needed. Because what we track and measure grows.

With how big the online world is becoming, many are forgetting the importance of events. Social media can enhance your lead generation and sponsoring events still create that necessary bond and comradery. As they mentioned, "leaders are born at events." Whenever your company or team has a large event, promoting that event should become your main focus. One of the best ways to amplify your efforts is to have as many team members as possible at those big events. There is a magic to them that can't be explained. It is one of the top ways I build my business, and nothing will ever replace that feeling of a big event. Trust us and focus on the big events!

Author: Torsten Sedlmeier

- Network Marketing Legend, with thirty years of experience, and was personally trained by Mr. Jim Rohn himself and other Top-Trainers like Tony Robbins.

- Since 2019 he has been a member of the "Next Level Mastermind Group" from Eric Worre. Throughout his career, he made it five times to the top, and had his ups and downs from being broke to becoming a seven-figure-income earner.

- Built teams of 50k+, and is a hard worker, supports and coaches his teams at the best, so 80 percent of his leaders never have been in Network Marketing or never have been successful in this industry before.

- His mission is to impact the lives of one million+ people for a BETTER life, by teaching his teams strategies and principles, how to build a big, profitable, sustainable and long-lasting business.

"It is not about the million dollars. It is about the million-dollar mindset and skill set that you are getting in network marketing."

-Jim Rohn

hear the same question all the time, "What do I do to be successful in this industry?" I remember asking one of my first sponsors this same question. I want you to know right from the start, that people may have answers for you. This book is going to have some direction for you to take. But none of it matters if you don't take ownership of what you are doing. The number one thing that you need to realize is that ownership is on you.

My first upline sponsor told me exactly what to do, and I followed it exactly. But I had no success at all. I went back to him and said, "I can't do this anymore." I was doing the actions, but I had no ownership of the actions. It turns out they were using me to test strategies out to see if it would be successful enough to tell their other people. They had used me for their own gain. It was at that moment that I realized I hadn't taken ownership of MY own business. I had blindly looked to someone else to tell me what to do without taking ownership of why I was doing those things.

I decided I wouldn't ever do anything else blindly in my business again. I would go and listen; I would go and train with the best. But I wasn't willing to do it blindly. I would decide what was best for me. I would take ownership of my business and do what was best for me. Look at the systems and tools that I and others are sharing in this book and decide what is going to work best for you.

Coaches Notes: I first met Torsten at my good friend Frazer Brooke's event in the U.K. This was a generic event. As I started talking with Torsten, I asked him how long he had been in network marketing. When I found out that he had thirty years of experience and was still attending events to learn, I was very impressed. Torsten has reached the top of five companies because he gets it. He stays humble, is always learning and is focused. I love his last line in the above paragraph. "Look at the systems and tools that I and others are sharing in this book and decide what is going to work best for you." This is crucial to your success because you can`t implement everything that you are learning in this book. Sometimes content can be so good that we get overwhelmed and never execute anything that we learn. Remember to take the most important strategies and then decide on the one you are going to focus on. Once you achieve that you can move on to the next most important strategy for your business.

Mentorship Worth It

That may sound like I am telling you not to listen or follow systems. It is the exact opposite of what I am saying. I am saying that you need to own the decisions you are making. Find and work with people that you want to listen to. Getting mentorship and personal development is one of the best things about this business, and you don't want to miss out on it.

Come in for the mentorship. One of the reasons that I signed up with the sponsor I am with right now is because of who the person was sponsored by. The upline was a woman that had made an 8-figure income in the industry. I wanted her to be my mentor. I knew how to become a seven-figure earner, but I didn't know how to take it to the next level.

Look for someone who is where you want to be. It doesn't have to be your direct sponsor. It can be someone else in the company, or it could be a coach like Rob Sperry. You have to be mentored by the person. I wanted this woman to teach me the last 2 percent that could help me leverage her knowledge to get me to the next level. Find the mentor that is doing the things that you want to be doing. Get in with them and own that you can learn a lot from mentors, coaches, and/or sponsors.

Coaches Notes: As Torsten said, "Find a mentor." Find someone who has done what you want to do. Find someone who will push you. Think about this. Even the greats have a mentor. The best athletes in the world find mentors to help them. Do not be scared to find a mentor. This is one of the most important keys to success. This is one of the main reasons that I hold masterminds. It gives people a chance to network, get to know different people at the events, different speakers, and find mentors that they can trust and go to.

Before You Even Start

Maybe some of you haven`t started network marketing yet, you may be switching companies, or really new to the business. I want to encourage you to do one thing before you start. If you are in a product-based industry, you have to be a testimony of your product.

I knew in my gut that my company was the next step for me. But before I signed up, I had to do one more thing. I had to test the product first. This is huge for product-based network marketing businesses. I had someone tell me a few days ago, "I don`t care what you are selling, the business looks good." NO! That is not how this works.

You must love the product that you are selling. I don`t want someone that is only the business guy, that is not willing to be all in with the company and product. 50% of our business is people that love the product and stay because of the product. But 50% come because of the business and stay for the product. It is important that you stand behind the company, product, or service that you are offering. I was buying the product, using it, and getting my own testimonial from the results I was having. Be your first testimonial. Love your product and believe in it, because it shows in how you are presenting.

When I started with this company, they weren`t even open in Europe yet, so I had to think internationally. I put in a lot of work and effort, but so worth it. And more and more people fell in love with the products and the opportunity and more and more customers had amazing results with the products. So, in a very short period of time, my community grew to 12.000+ people. As a result, I achieved one of the highest ranks and it is just the beginning. I could do that because I was a testimony of the product. I was my first customer and I recruited people that were their own first customers. That means I have created a business full of people who believe in the product, and that shows up in the sales! Many came because of the product, but stayed because of the business opportunity as well. Putting in hard work, focusing on getting "raving fans of the products" as a customer base is the best way, building a big, profitable and sustainable business.

Know What You Are Getting Paid On

One mistake that people make in the beginning is not knowing what they are getting paid on. You are getting paid on the value that you bring to the marketplace. Recruiting is part of sales. Most people don`t see it that way, but recruiting is selling your opportunity to do the business.

I see people getting stuck on the word "selling" We are always selling. We don`t think about it that way, but we are. We are selling our kids to go to bed at bedtime or to eat their vegetables. We are selling ideas. We sell ourselves and our personalities all of the time. Everyone does sales every single day, but we don`t see it that way. Everyone`s in sales and we are selling every single day. People are afraid of sales, but it is nothing to be afraid of.

All business is communication and relationship building. Some people try to skip this, and they try to spam you and don`t build anything. C`mon! No one wants this. I get these messages daily.

Go back to always selling. How well does it go with your child if you spam them about a product when you are trying to sell them on going to bed? It won`t work to sell the bed! You must sell for the gain or pain and not the product. People are spamming, people are going out and telling people fabrications about the product or the company. The truth is good enough! Network marketing is not perfect. But it is the best thing out there for the average person to build a business with the lowest cost and the lowest risk. You can keep your regular job and if you do it long enough, your income from network marketing will increase. Use your selling skills and sell people on the real product, the real opportunity and see how you can solve their gain or pain with your offer.

Know Your Audience

I live in Europe and people ask me how to grow an international team. My number one thing that I tell people is learn about the culture you are going into. Respect the culture of people. You have to respect the culture that people are coming from. You need to understand that people are going to be recruited differently in the US than they will be in other parts of the world.

For instance, here in Europe, we are more skeptical people of things like network marketing. People over here are going to ask you a lot of questions and they are going to take their time figuring out and looking into things. The US market is very quick on fire, but that fire can burn out quickly with Americans. You have to be willing to move quickly in the US market. It is completely different in Europe. They have to get all of the information first and do their investigation. Respect the culture!

I almost didn`t sign up with my sponsor because they didn`t understand why I had so many questions. We started talking and they kind of blew off my questions. In our first short conversation, they found out that I was successful in network marketing and the more questions I would ask, the more they would blow them off or give short quick answers.

They didn`t know that I was looking to change companies. Always be ready to share information and be willing to share it with everyone. Never prejudge if someone is interested or not in your offer.

For two months, I kept asking questions and trying to get information that would help me learn more about their company, their products, and the compensation plan. I kept getting insignificant answers.

Respect someone and give them time. Never presume. There were eight top earners that I met, and they all presumed, but each and every one could have signed me up, if they would have just respected the culture where I am coming from and would have answered all my questions. The person I finally signed up with didn`t recruit me. I recruited myself, like I mentioned before, because of who the person was sponsored by. In this short period of time, my team is already one of the biggest teams in my sponsor`s business. You never know who is open and who is not. Don`t presume, ever. Treat everyone nice and equal and respect their culture.

Trust Your Numbers

I love numbers because they tell a story about business. If you aren`t a numbers person, no worries! But I want you all to have some numbers about the business so that we can see the story that it creates about your own business and about network marketing.

There are three phases to this business. In phase one, you put in two thirds of the work, but you only get paid one third. The second phase you put in fifty percent of the work, and you get paid fifty percent. The third phase is putting in one third of the work and getting paid two thirds. Most people never even get to phase two. Because they drop out in the first phase.

I don`t want you to have a false expectation in this business. I also don`t want you creating false expectations. The average lifespan in network marketing is ninety days. Across the board with every single company. People are shocked by this number. If I sign up someone, there is a good chance that they won`t be here in ninety days. This is good information for you to know. Because when we know the numbers, we can see what we can do to change the numbers in your business. And there is a way to extend someone`s lifespan in this business. You can get someone to stay in network marketing for an average for one hundred and eighty days if you do this one thing.

If you help someone make passive income of a minimum of one dollar. Doesn`t matter how much, but if you can help them make any money in network marketing in the first ninety days, you can extend their lifespan in this business to one hundred and eighty days or beyond. It helps people see what could happen.

In the first ninety days you need to get into their social network. Because it is most likely that he or she may not be there. You don`t want to miss out on their social network. I never run out of contacts because of this. I am always trying to get connections through people that have just signed up. I make it really easy. They find the people and open a three-way chat on What`s App or Messenger. Easy. They get the conversation started and I take it from there. They may drop out, but I now have relationships with their network. Ask people "who are their three to five most business-oriented people they know?" They are the people that I am going to focus on. I never run out of people to contact. This is a basic principle that works. It is easier than ever with social media.

Let`s look at some more numbers around recruiting. Seventy percent are actually deemed as "Consumers". They use a product, but they really have no intention of building a business. Twenty percent are considered "Social Enrollers." That means they will enroll one to two people casually over their lifetime in their business. Five percent are considered "Retailers". They`re all about the product! They may recruit three to five business partners while they are in the business, but they`re mostly focused on retailing. Three percent are considered "Recruiters" and enroll six to nine personally sponsored people over the life of their business. And the Top two percent those are the ones we called the "Super Recruiters". They enroll ten or more people in the lifetime of their business. Those "Super Recruiters" are responsible for a full seventy percent of everybody that ever signs up in network marketing. Can you believe that!?! By the way: The average super recruiter will sign up twenty seven people in their lifetime of network marketing. If they are doing their whole career with an average of twenty-seven people, how crazy is that?!

Let`s break that down. If you are the newest person in network marketing and you sponsor a new person every single month, in one year, you will have twelve people that you have sponsored. You are a super recruiter. Here is the problem: I see this happening after the first year in their business. People go into management mode. And monkey see, monkey do, their teams do the same thing. It gets smaller and smaller. After the first year of recruiting, eight of those people will drop out, and you will be left with four. If you still don`t recruit by year two, you will only be left with one person. You must keep recruiting! This is the fact.

The next year, if you want to have the same income, and you know, eight people are checking out, you must recruit eight people. If you want a bigger business, you need to recruit more. If you are active, most people won`t see the results the first year. You will see the results are delayed. Don`t let the delay make you fall off with your work. You must work the business, even if the results aren`t seen right now. Don`t trust yourself, trust the numbers that you are getting.

If you had ten people that you recruited, you will find something really interesting with the recruits. You will have one person that will do this business with or without you. They are the rockstars. You will have two to three people that do it with a part time mentality. A couple more will just be doing business by accident. They love the product, they love the community, and they love to hang out inside the business. The rest will be the people that do nothing.

You will want to know what category people fall into so that you know where to spend your time. Don`t get stuck spending all your time with business by accident. There is nothing that says that your first ten recruits will fall exactly into this number ratio. You may sign up your first ten people and they may all be in the nothing category. You may even see that your first thirty to fifty people are just here for you to get to know how to learn to recruit. Save your best recruits for when you have practiced a bit or get your successful upline involved BEFORE you contact them, so your upline can help and show you how to do it the right way.

If you sign up one hundred people, think about what your numbers will look like!? You will have approximately ten people that are self-motivated and rockstars. You never know when they will come, but they will be there. But, you need to sign up at least one hundred people! Trust the numbers!

I believe that everyone is recruitable. Every single person. I believe this. But not anytime, and not from everybody. Go back and ask yourself what you can learn and find a mentor or a coach. Know where you are getting paid from and sell the company or product from a place of belief. Be respectful of people and their culture, build relationships with them, and work hard so that you can help enough people to be successful for themselves and reach their goals; you will reach your goals. Focus on that and the universe will provide.

Coaches Notes: I wish I would have had this training early on in my network marketing career. I tried to fit everyone into my goals rather than follow Torsten`s advice and love people where they are. I didn`t realize that some people just love the community while others want to make a little extra money. My goals were so high that I only focused on what I wanted. I pushed so many people out of the business with that style. It took me several years to learn that amateurs convince while experts sift and sort. Once I learned this I could make everyone feel important and whatever level they wanted to participate. This created a stronger culture and much better retention.

Author: Kaylee Siber

- Seven Star Director with my current company holding a leadership position on the committee.

- Have helped hundreds of people`s dreams of financial freedom come true.

- Created a community of over three hundred thousand called Starfish Crusaders

- Donate ten percent of my income back to help kids that have aged out of foster care that still need assistance and want to go to school.

- Continue to learn and grow every day so I can be a better leader for my team.

"I already know what giving up feels like. I want to see what happens if I don't."

Fortune is in the follow up, but only if you do it. Previous to doing network marketing, I built houses. I took people through the process from dirt on a lot to putting the last doorknob on. My entire business was built on continuous follow up with my customer. It was daily check-ins and seeing how the build was going, how they were feeling about it, and if there needed to be any changes.

I learned a lot about follow up doing that business that translated to network marketing. Because follow up is going to be the same regardless of what type of industry you are in. When I talk about follow up, I am talking about getting in contact with someone who is either an existing customer or someone who has expressed interest in the product or business.

Follow up can be done across different social media platforms, phone, text, email, and in person. My preferred method of follow up is on Facebook and on Facebook messenger.

When you first start this business, you are going to want to reach out to everybody. But what happens after you have done that? I found for myself that I had to reach back out not just to new people, but I needed to do the same thing as my old house building business and follow up with the people that were in my business.

Following up with your current clients, customers, and business associates is key. These are people that already said yes to the opportunity. These are people that have already invested in the product. These are people that are interested in doing more. Take the best care of the people that are already in your business.

If you aren`t following up with the people who know, like, trust, and purchased from you, then you are losing money. If you keep the customers happy, they will literally go and find new people for you.

Especially for people that are doing this business part time, follow up with your customers. When you do this, it helps them see that you are dedicated to them and they will stick around. Make sure they will get what you told them they would.

Coaches Notes: I still remember a few years ago hosting my first mastermind with top leaders. Kaylee was at this mastermind. She gave one of the best tips for how she built her business. She stayed in touch with others. She briefly mentioned that her key to following up was to stay in daily contact. That is one of the huge benefits of attending masterminds. You are able to meet, connect, and stay connected with people like Kaylee. Kaylee focuses on this aspect of staying in touch even before prospecting and well after prospecting. Every three months she goes through every person on her FB, which is maxed out on friends, and she sends them a message via FB messenger. This message isn`t her pitch message. I am talking about Kaylee just simply being a good human and staying in touch with others. This simple tip has now been implemented by several other top leaders and had a profound impact on their business growth.

Three Types Of Follow Up

There are three types of systems I use when following up. The first is for the person that has expressed interest and hasn`t yet purchased or joined the business.

Create a group where anyone that is interested can join. This helps keep everyone in one place. Once they have become a customer, they can stay in the group. This helps so that you have lots of people in the group, and your current customers can share about how they like the product.

I like to keep my group as a place for people to ask questions, get help, share successes, and stay up to date on what is new with my team and the company. If people express interest in the product, I invite them to join the group.

Once they join the group, I send them a message in messenger to let them know I personally saw that they are in the group and I am excited to have them here. From there, I engage with prospects in messenger if they message me. I do engagement with them in the Facebook group. This helps keep everyone engaged and active in the group, and I can answer one question that one person may have asked, but several people want to know the answer to.

The group is a place to keep people easily in one area.

Money is made in messenger. And fortune really is in follow up...if you do it. Once someone is my customer I have a seven-day follow up system. I follow up in messenger on days one, two, three, five, and seven. Some people may think it is too much. But I found that in this industry, you have to be there and support people. If you let a day go by in the first couple of days without following up and answering questions, you could lose someone. This enables me to talk with them about what they are loving, and also get to ask them questions about their goals, personal life, etc. so I can start to establish a better connection with them.

I follow up personally with my customers individually that first week and then they go into the Facebook group. I have a great platform that they go into where I can follow up with them as a group after that first week. I continue the follow up in the group at fourteen, twenty-one, and thirty days. After that, I follow up with them every single month. I never do it the week that their autoship comes out. I don`t ever want my customers to think they are just a number to me. I always follow up the week before or after.

You have to get personal with people and touch them where their heartbeat is. If you don`t, it will be hard to keep them. You have to be willing to get to know people.

I have an initial questionnaire that I ask people to fill out as soon as they sign up and order products. I always want to know when they start and when they get their product. I then stay connected with them.

I do most of my follow ups at night because that is when people are at home. People have the same problems. They just express them in a different way. You have to be good at listening to the problem and then talk to them about it. I also want to know how the problems are affecting their personal lives. People want instant gratification that includes following up.

The biggest obstacle that people face with follow up is getting a tracking system that enables them to know who to follow up with, what to follow up about, where to follow up and how to engage with them. Create your who, what, where, and how tracking system to help you know.

I have a master list that I use that enables me to track easily who needs to be followed up with. I write every single thing down that I talk to the customer about. I write down their goals, their reasons to try the product, their why. If you follow the system and stay consistent, persistent, and patient, you will get there.

The third follow up system I use is for my business associates that are starting the business with me. I have a seven-day approach with anyone that has joined the business. We have a seven-day launch that helps us track where people are at and help them stay motivated. I truly believe that if you can keep people engaged and willing for seven days, they will do this business for thirty days. If you keep them motivated for thirty days, they will do it for ninety days and so on. The longer you help them be happy and motivated, the longer they will stay with you.

Coaches Notes: The main principles that Kaylee is teaching here are to be consistent with following up and make sure you TRACK IT. Everyone has a different system for tracking. Some like digital whereas others love writing it by hand. The main point is to track it and then put it in your calendar. This is your business and you need to treat it like a business. You never know which person you potentially sponsor that could change everything for you.

Customers Are Your Recruits

Your customers are your recruiters. I send a thank you card to every single person that places an order with me. People love handwritten cards. I get messages all of the time where people tell me that they can`t remember the last time they got a handwritten letter. I send a three-month gift for every single person that orders for three consistent months with me. Those are the people that I am constantly following up with. The people I really want to take care of are the people who are already here. It is much easier to keep a customer then to go and get new ones. Recruit your customers by taking care of them. It is the same with team members, as well.

The first year that people sign up as my customers, they get nineteen "touches" from me. I call it the sticky tape method. The more contact like birthday messages, happy Monday messages, reach out and say hello. The stickier tape it is, the more they will become wrapped up in you, and they won`t go to anyone else. They are only going to go to you because you have spent the time. It teaches about follow up and how important it is.

Follow up is huge. Follow up with your customers. I ask people how much attention they may need from me. I want them to know that I am here, I write it down and use my calendar a lot. It took me a while to get to my phone. I also keep a notebook. The more you know your customers, the more you can keep them on the product and keep them engaged. Find out the information openly. It just comes across as a conversation on messenger.

So many people have gotten away from email marketing. I send an email to anyone that signs up with me. I send a monthly newsletter to all my customers. It helps to keep me and my business top of mind for people. Some people may think email marketing is dead, but it isn't. I personally will open emails from people that I have bought things from. If you stay consistent it makes a difference. It is one more way to contact people.

Even old customers that have been with me for years will tell me how much they still are with me because I stay connected with them.

I would much rather have fifty people that order from me every single month than try and get fifty new people every month that I can't keep. It is easy to keep people when you follow up.

I talk to my customer about how they can share this with their friends and family through the business. If they don't want to do that, I give them the option of making a post that I give them on their personal page and tagging me in it so their friends and family know who to come to. This has been hugely successful and most people are happy to do that. I have done a lot of follow up by this time, and they trust me. I have the person that made the post put me and the person interested in a messenger group together. That way, it creates the connection immediately. I have them introduce me, "This is my friend Kaylee she is the one that got me this product and she is excited to get you started." They always say, "This is my friend..." Once they say that, it creates third party validation. I then go back to the person that made the post and double check that they don't want to do this business and remind them about the perks of joining in the business before I sign any of their friends and family up as customers. Your customers are your biggest recruits. Take care of them, and they will help take care of your business.

Why Follow Up

Retention will keep your business thriving. I have a sixty seven percent retention rate in my business. People don`t believe that I have these retention numbers. It all comes from follow up and keeping up with people.

The one question I get the most about following up is, "What do you do when you reach out and people don`t message you back?"

Don`t let it bother you. Let people be people. I have people not respond all the time. I used my follow up system with one of my customers and she never messaged me back. Not once. A couple months in she posted in the Facebook group what a huge success she had using the product and how much she loved it. If I would have made it personal that she wasn`t messaging me back, I may have lost a happy customer. You never know why people aren`t getting back. It doesn`t really matter. Keep to the system. Follow up even with people that have stopped two years ago. You never know when they will come back. I never remove people from my group. I say you have to die or delete me.

This business is one of the most wonderful opportunities for anyone to make a little money or a lot of money. It is always up to them. If you want to keep the momentum going in your business, follow up. Because fortune really is in the follow up.

Coaches Notes: What a powerful paragraph from Kaylee. "Your customers are your recruiters. I send a thank you card to every single person that places an order with me. People love handwritten cards. I get messages all of the time where people tell me that they can`t remember the last time they got a handwritten letter. I send a three month gift for every single person that orders for three consistent months with me. Those are the people that I am constantly following up with. The people I really want to take care of are the people who are already here. It is much easier to keep a customer then to go and get new ones. Recruit your customers by taking care of them. It is the same with team members as well."

Customers are the lifeblood of real sustainable business. You want to recruit more business builders? Having a strong customer acquisition and retention will attract business builders. You want to have more business builders? Many of your customers will either become business builders or they will lead you to their business builders. You have a gold mine sitting right in front of you with your current and future customers. Make sure to go the extra mile and take care of them. They will in return take care of you and help you build your empire.

Author: Judy Stallings

- Full Time Network Marketer since 2013

- $5 Million+ earned in less than 3.5 years

- Earned 2 Seven Figure Earner rings

- Two time published author

- 2020 Inductee in the Network Marketing Million Dollar Hall of Fame

- Top 1% in her company

- Holds record earning highest rank in company in less than 10 months

"Dreams don't work unless you do."

— John C. Maxwell

Team Average of $3 Million in Sales Monthly

I`m what you might call an "accidental network marketer". I never set out to be known as a network marketer, in fact I resisted it for years. I always compared network marketers to used car salesmen, always hyping up their opportunity. This never sat well with me.

Over the last several years, I have learned there are many ways to recruit people to my organization. Because I learned what worked for me and how I could impact lives, I am now proud to call myself a Network Marketer, and it was no accident!

In my opinion, there`s no right or wrong way to recruit people into your business. We are all different - we are not shaped from the exact same mold. We each have our own unique personality, emotions, desires and dreams. What works for one will not work for all.

To be successful in this business, you must find what works for you. I think one of the biggest mistakes a leader can make is expecting others to do things their way. I have my way of building my business, and it`s what I teach, but I encourage everyone to learn from other leaders and coaches. I know my way of doing things may not be the ticket for them. I`m not everyone`s cup of tea, which is why I totally stand behind anyone who wants to learn from other leaders and coaches.

Before I give out advice, let me give you a little background on my Network Marketing experience.

I first learned about direct sales marketing when I was in my mid-20s, working a full-time job as well as a part time job as a cocktail waitress at an upscale fitness club. One night at the bar, the manager walked in with a product kit from a new company. Somehow, he convinced several of us to sign up and pay over $300 for the kit, because "it would change our lives." I bought into the hype he spewed, thinking it was my ticket out of working my life away.

Where did things go wrong? Why didn`t I become rich and successful? These are questions I asked myself. But I now know the issue was a lack of understanding of how the business model worked. No one took the time to educate me, so I was left feeling like a failure. Incidentally, this company is still going strong 30 years later - imagine what I could have done if I only had the knowledge and the tools to be successful.

Years went by and I would jump into several companies. Nothing changed, because I didn`t change. I still had no idea what I was doing or what this business was all about, but I knew it was possible to be successful. Sadly, I had no idea how to go about it.

Back in those days, we didn`t have social media. I am not sure I could have accomplished what I have without social media. Being an introvert, the arrival of social media opened up many doors. In 2011, I gave it another shot. For the first time ever, I realized that it`s not just about recruiting. While that is a very important key to success, it`s not the only way. I tried to recruit for an entire year and nothing clicked. But I stood behind the product and started sharing it. This led to customers, which led to them becoming distributors. Before I knew it, I had a downline full of average people just like me. We were sharing our testimonials and love for our product and it changed our lives.

After 6.5 years, it was time for me to move on. I had a case of Network Marketing PTSD. Although business was amazing for the first three years or so, things changed, and it was time to do something else with my life. I didn`t think it would be another NM company.

I have been with my current company for over three years. What drew me to it was a product that I had been looking into. The fact that I could try this product and earn commission if I referred others was a plus. I joined without having any intentions of building another team, but I was excited about the product. So, that night I did a live video on Facebook talking about my new venture and the products. That video spawned a series of events that happened so quickly, I sometimes look back on it and still can`t believe it.

Over the next month, I sponsored more than 100 new affiliates and had countless new customers. Within six months, I crushed seven out of eight ranks with only one to go. In less than 10 months I hit that highest rank - since that time, my company has added another rank which is still waiting to be claimed.

Everyone asked me, "What is your secret?" The truth is, there is no secret. I am about to share with you some recruiting tips that have worked for me in acquiring new customers as well as team members.

Coaches Notes: I love being around Judy! Judy came to one of my seven figure masterminds and was such an asset to the group. She is about to drop some incredible strategies, but first, let`s learn from some of the principles she just taught us in her story. She mentioned how she switched companies many times always thinking things would be different but they never were. Things didn`t change until she took responsibility. Jim Rohn says it best, "Don`t wish it were easier, Wish you were better." Taking 100 percent responsibility is far more important than any strategies you will learn, which is exactly why Judy started there. Mindset will eat skills and systems for breakfast. This business takes time and you need to make sure you allow yourself to learn and grow - which begins with you taking responsibility.

It's All about Relationships

Network Marketing is Relationship Marketing. Think about it, without people who need our opportunity or product, we have no team/customers. After my miserable year of trying to recruit and I only earned seven hundred dollars in an entire year. My sister Jackie and I were talking about quitting, when she said how much she loved the product but not so much the recruiting aspect. We realized we could build a business focusing on customers and for us recruiting was not the way to go. I shifted my focus and started focusing on the product that I believed in and sharing it with my social media friends and followers. I also learned that people aren't just going to buy it because I shared it. They had to trust me. Building trust was a long process. Those relationships didn't come overnight.

How do you build long lasting relationships? You talk to people and show them you truly care about their wellbeing. I have used Facebook for years to build my relationships. Being authentic is crucial - people can see through it if you aren't genuine. Be a person that you would follow. Be positive and share valuable content that makes people want to follow your page.

Cultivate your relationships daily and make new friends who share your interests. I'm not saying that everyone you communicate with is going to buy your product or join your team, but you are building trust. When the time comes that they have a need, they will remember you as the person they want to join or purchase from.

Walk the Walk, Don't just Talk the Talk

The only way to be authentic about your product or opportunity is to believe in it yourself. Could you imagine promoting something that you wouldn`t genuinely want to tell your best friends or family about? Part of building trust is working with companies and products that you stand behind 100 percent.

I joined my current company because of the product. Originally, I only wanted to purchase the product to help my dog with some issues. What I found along the way, though, was how many lives I could positively impact.

I think too many people get into business with only the bottom line in mind. They don`t care what the product is as long as the comp plan pays out. In my experience, I have found that some of the best team members are people who originally bought the product, loved it, and wanted to share it with others.

Bottom line - find a company with products and culture that you can stand behind.

Develop a Positive Mindset

Mindset is everything! Not only do you have to believe in yourself, you have to love yourself. You can`t love yourself and help others if you have a negative mindset.

Positivity didn`t come natural to me. I wasn`t the most positive person back in 2011. I would even say I was quite negative. I was a pessimistic person all my life. I thought if something bad was going to happen, I would much rather plan for it than be positive and have it knock the wind out of my sails. One day, I had a wakeup call. By being negative, I was attracting negative. I had to intentionally work on being positive.

It wasn`t always easy, but now it just comes naturally. You have to be grateful for what you have and not focus on what you don`t have.

When I started to use my social media to spread positivity and good content, people started sharing my posts. I started getting friend requests and followers. Many became team members or customers.

Don't Treat Your Social Media Profile as an Advertisement

I believe one of the biggest mistakes you can make on social media is being one big commercial. Too many people join a company and immediately begin to spam all over their page. People fast forward through commercials, and they will do the same with your page. They will unfollow you if you don`t provide value.

To make true connections with people, let them see who you are and what makes you tick. Share your life and positive content.

Every morning I start the day with something inspirational. You never know what people are going through, and your post could make all the difference for them. I can`t count how many times I`ve received messages from followers telling me it was just what they needed.

I typically stay away from posting anything negative or controversial. You are going to attract what you are putting out there. I got away from negativity years ago, and it`s not a place I want to revisit.

Don`t be afraid to step out of your comfort zone. You have to reach out and meet new people. Make new friends every single day. You can`t just post about your company and product and think that people will come. You have to build your online presence first. Build those friendships and increase your following. Then when you do make the occasional business post, they will see it.

Coaches Notes: This is a big key! Your social media is to connect with other people. Your goal is to provide value to them, not to be a SPAMMER. Spammers are always annoying. Think of your favorite commercials. They don`t just come on and pitch you. They provide value even if it is something humorous. It is called SOCIAL media and spam media for a reason. It is great to standout on social media, but do it in a way that fits your style and personality. Do it in a way that provides value. Learn how to add value and stop spamming with *The Game of Networking*.

Don't Give up too Quickly

Success isn't a given, and it's not automatic. You have to work. You have to put in the time. Anyone who joins network marketing with the belief they will have overnight success will never stay long enough to see it. You need to see it as a two to five year plan. So what if it takes five years to make five figures a month? That's more than most people earn working 40 to 60 hours a week. Consider the alternative - work a job until you are old enough to retire and possibly get a party and a gold watch?

This business is not easy, but it is fun and rewarding, but you have to give it time. Don't compare yourself to others. You might be at the beginning of your journey, while they are in the middle of theirs. Like you, they had to start fresh.

People get into network marketing without thinking about their long-term plan. Most are looking for a quick payout, but they forget this is a relationship building business and relationships take time. Play for the long-term game, and not the short-term game.

Set up your business, your social media, and your life so that people can follow you, get to know you, and interact with you.

There are many ways to recruit people to your business. The tips I have given are just what has worked for me. Network Marketing is truly a relationship business. Spend the time creating honest connections with people.

With the current state of the world, many people are lonely and sad. In this digital age we are more connected than ever. When you can be a bright light and message of positivity in someone`s life, a relationship may begin. Build from there and continue to spread the positivity. Your business will grow, because you have grown, and you are changing people`s lives. And that is what I have found is worth more than money can buy.

Besides all the amazing friends I have met through Network Marketing, I have to say the greatest thing to happen for me is I have realized my worth. I don`t think I ever found self-confidence until I was able to help change people`s lives. While I am still a bit introverted, I am finding myself more confident to step out into new horizons - just past the place that I`m comfortable. And I have to give Rob Sperry a big shout out for this. Attending his Mastermind changed my life.

If I can do this business and be successful, I promise you can, too!

Coaches Notes: People are attracted to energy! Think about the people in your life you love being around vs the people you dread being around. It is all about the energy they have. That energy starts with your outlook and positive mindset. We all have setbacks but how you choose to look at those setbacks will determine everything. Judy didn`t have success in several companies but she kept the right mindset and pushed forward until she became one of the top earners in our profession.

Authors: Annie And Charlie Starky

- Built a multiple seven-figure MLM business with many multiple six to seven figure earners on their team.

- In the same company over nineteen years.

- Stay/work at home parents for three kids their entire education

- Family is our Why and not our excuse.

- Purchased the Dream farm again and now living and loving life on our terms.

'The same wind blows on us all; the winds of disaster, opportunity and change. Therefore, it is not the blowing of the wind, but setting of the Sails that will determine our direction in life.'

- *Jim Rohn*

Brave Enough, Bold Enough!

We had been prospected before, but it wasn`t until some major life events happened to us that we really opened up to the possibility of network marketing. The first time our neighbor invited us to see the business opportunity of network marketing, we were on a cattle and sheep property that was over 65,000 acres and very time consuming. A major drought hit our locality and we were struggling in many areas.

(Annie) My neighbor, also on a large property, asked me to look at a business opportunity. I sat and listened and thought it was exciting and had great potential. When I got back from town and shared my excitement with Charlie on the farm, he told me I could order a bit of product if I wanted, but was totally dismissive and was too busy to hear anything about it. As much as I thought it was a great opportunity, we were so caught up in the drama of the drought that we couldn`t even think about it any further. Unfortunately, as the months rolled on, we got more engrossed in our dire situation. Eventually the banks came and foreclosed on us. We were forced to sell our property and walk away with very little.

Three and a half years later from that first exposure, that same neighbor came back and followed up with us again. She was brave enough to have the conversation in the beginning and was bold enough to follow up with us a fair while later. That is why we are here today living our dream life. She didn`t know what was going on with us at the first visit, but she was willing to have the conversation with us in the beginning and in the following years.

We were open. It was time. We didn`t hesitate the second time. We had a business mindset before with Annie`s previous corporate background and with running the ranch, but our thinking wasn`t open to more until it was crunch time. The wind of disaster was definitely blowing on us. We finally became open to more, and we decided to set our sails with the wind rather than against it. We knew we didn`t want an average life, so we decided to give it a good shot.

From day one in MLM, we were going to do it together as a team and do it for five years, consistently and solidly. We gave ourselves a five-year period to be able to really build with serious intent and not question any processes or results. The entrepreneur business model and structure made sense, and we believed that if we gave it our best shot, we could achieve something special. In reality, it worked in seven months. We then knew we would be 'lifetimers` in this phenomenal industry.

> **Coaches Notes:** There are two huge sentences that stood out to me. "From day one in MLM, we were going to do it together as a team and do it for five years, consistently and solidly. We gave ourselves a five year period to be able to really build with serious intent and not question any processes or results." One of the biggest mistakes that network marketers make is claiming to be committed, but then they quit after a couple of months. Of course, it didn`t work for them because they were never truly committed. They never treated their network marketing business like a REAL BUSINESS. Charlie and Annie were both featured speakers at one of my events in Australia. They are as humble and coachable as you will ever see, especially considering they are top earners with loads of experience. They were committed to their business and dreams from day one and their success followed that commitment.

SIX areas of FOLLOW UP - critical for all success

Follow up is an entire process and absolutely critical when you first get started. You will often hear fortune is in the follow - up, because it is.

We teach six areas of follow up and we believe it is something you need to learn how to do well. If you are serious about building your dream life, you will dedicate three or more hours a day to building this business and follow up is a major part.

The six areas of follow up we teach:

- Prospects (people who are on your list and who you are actively recruiting for customer or business),

- Recruits (people who are in your pipeline and with whom you are in current dialogue).

- Distributors (those that you are assisting with their building process and coaching),

- Customers (recently joined and learning about the product ranges).

- Inactive customers or builders (those who have joined and not yet doing much with the business),

- Business builders (leaders whom you enjoy some leverage with and yet independent).

We follow up with people that say yes and no. We are always following up and continuing to make and keep connections and conversations happening. Following up is literally the business we are in!

The follow up in each area is for thirty minutes each day and obviously depends at what stage your business is in. To achieve follow up in an ordered structure like this, it is critical that you are consistent and organized. You have to be transparent and clear at the start of each conversation, whether by phone or message, that it`s a quick process. For example, when I was following up with a very busy real estate agency owner whom I was prospecting for business, I kept it quick... "The reason for my call is to touch base and just let you know I haven`t forgotten you or our original conversation, and let`s connect when you are not so busy". It is not a hard core conversation or pressure, but it was letting him know I am still invested and will keep up the contact until we get a decision to move forward. Follow up can be so quick. (This real estate agent is now in our business and sending referrals to us).

To be really effective and efficient in our business, we encourage our leaders to work in 30-minute blocks of time in the six areas of follow up. That way, no one can get lost in the process of building. An excellent tracker system and diary is also critical so the opportunity to forward plan who is next on your follow up lists is advised. We also encourage a six point list of what must be achieved before retiring the next night... The Razor`s Edge activity sheet. This ensures revenue-raising activities are enacted each day. Some people now call the activity Daily Method of Operation which is great, but the key is not to hide in one area or run out of time by using procrastination or delay tactics.

People often want guiding scripts, and usually leaders can provide these to you. The key is to just be you - be authentic and natural in your speech and demeanor and always smile in every conversation whether it be a voice message, text or a phone follow- up. Your vibration is everything. Never be needy or desperate, or even rushed. Your prospects, customers, and recruits will pick up on your vibration. I often follow up while I am making dinner. This is beneficial not only for me, as I have a time limit, but for whoever I am following up with, as well. I will say something like, "Hi Julie, I wanted to have a quick catch up while I`ve got the peas on. I have about five minutes. Can you talk............?" Most people are so happy because they only have five minutes, too. They don`t want to be on a catch up call for too long. I do the same with a message on messenger... "Hi Carol, just a quick touch base before I shoot out... / or head to bed/ or start a zoom, ... How did you do with the presentation, and what did you like best about it? When`s a good time to connect voice to voice?"

Creating the boundaries around your time with follow up is HUGE!! Be specific about why you are talking to your contact. Set the time and set the expectation from the beginning. Let people know that you are going to be to the point. Otherwise, lonely people are just going to chat with you. 'The reason for my quick call is........` is always a good one.

Ninety percent of this business is follow up. Always book your next follow up from the current one you are in. It is always the next conversation. It makes it so easy even on direct message/ messenger. For example, "I hope this makes sense. We will chat about it tomorrow." People are expecting to hear from you. Let them know that you will be in touch. You aren`t going to ghost them. Be a connector.

One of the most important areas of success for us is in following up with customers or builders who have become inactive. We never know what is happening in the lives of anyone, so reaching out to Inactive customers and builders with caring conversations can make a difference. This is something that needs to be well thought out and planned but never pressured. Often answering simple questions and finding solutions can reactivate a customer account. It`s all about continuing your relationship and friendships. Helping a business builder re-engage is so exciting and so worth the caring call.

Education in our business is very important. We are in a Health and Wellness company, so it is important that we invest in educating our customers and answer questions about the product and their order. We know that we invest in their education, they will stay loyal and become raving fans of the product, company, and our business. That can possibly lead to them wanting to share their knowledge with family and friends and then becoming a business builder. Customers also provide the best leads with referrals! The old sales saying is 'the best customer you can have is the one you already do have` Follow up regularly. This area often needs more time than other areas, especially in the early days of building your network. Facebook Groups are now providing a fantastic medium for education and community engagement, and so much can be achieved in a few simple posts and tagging.

Coaches Notes: Most people don`t know this, but I was approached by eleven different network marketing companies, and I said no to every single one until finally joining in 2008. Each one of the first eleven network marketing companies who I was approached by never followed up with me. Now to be totally transparent, I never showed extreme interest, but that`s because I was scared they would try to hard close me. So, instead, I was very nonchalant about it. There were about four companies that I was very interested in, but again, they never followed up with me. I know I would have joined at least one or two had they just stayed in contact with me. I just didn`t want to make a decision right away. This six-step formula breaks it down to WHO you need to follow up, and you also just learned the most important principles of following up. DO NOT STOP FOLLOWING UP just because someone is nonchalant. I became the #1 recruiter out of a million distributors and could have been on someone else`s team years earlier had they only followed a system like Charlie and Annie laid out. Do not underestimate the power in the follow ups! Learn more about follow ups at www.sperrybonus.com

Don't Judge A Person
By Their Response

Don't ever judge other people. Look for potential and energy. When you see people who have good energy and presence, they may be a potential business builder for you. After a while you can sort of feel when people will be a great fit in your business. We both have a gift of being able to see people's potential even if they can't see it themselves. Someone saw it in us and was willing to pursue that. We see potential and just love the people where they are. People are going to be attracted to you just by your very being and your certainty about your business. Your energy is right, and you are supporting and encouraging.

We have a few prospects right now and we don't know if they will build with us. They don't have a full understanding yet of what's possible, but we see their potential and we will love them and just keep following up. Be a natural networker. That means having regular conversations with people. Follow Up. Check in with them and see how they are going every once in a while on a regular basis. Hang in there with them, and they may come. The message here is not to give up on anyone.

Even when your prospects say no, sometimes it's not really a no. It's not now, or not yet. Sometimes, the circumstances for them just aren't lining up. That is how it was for us when we were first invited to the opportunity. You have to be willing to continue to follow up for when the circumstances do line up. Be a friend. Support them in their lives. Be visible to them. Send business their way, if you can. Network with them and support them. Social media makes it so much easier today. Send quick messages of love and support.

Networking is networking regardless of what network or business you are in. Be organic and yet disciplined in your follow up and networking. The key is to be interested in them. You have heard it before, but people will not respond well and do business with you unless they know, like and trust you.... Trust can take a while to establish and develop. Give it a chance.

We had one woman that gave us a 'Yes I would like to build a business` a few months ago. I set up a time to catch up and talk and she didn`t show up. I thought it was interesting that she didn`t show, but that didn`t stop me from following up. I kept reaching out and connecting until she finally reached out months later and let us know that she was going through a tough time personally. Even though she wasn`t reaching out to us, we continually reached out and followed up with her. She was very appreciative. At the end of the day you never know what people are going through. There might be something we do or say that can help them in their life.

Set up a long term business. Network marketing isn`t just a short-term business. Your business isn`t going to be made of five, ten or fifteen people. If you play long-term, your team is going to be fifteen hundred, fifteen thousand or fifteen million and more. That`s when it gets really exciting, and you know you are a long-term player on a long-term team. Treat it like it is part of the process.... A long-term process with a long-term vision. Having a long-term vision with big goals and dreams that drive you to continue on even when the going gets tough is very important.

How Many Eggs Are In The Basket?

We always have a list of thirty names that we are actively recruiting. We advise at least thirty (this also keeps you out of management mode). If you are only trying to hatch one egg metaphorically, that is a problem. You will be so desperate to have that one hatch and your prospect will feel it. It is advisable to have thirty eggs that you are trying to hatch. You can work with thirty, and it`s exciting and vibrant. The odds are in your favor that one or several will hatch. When you have more names on your list/funnel, it gives you time to build relationships and assist them grow, develop, and "hatch" into your business.

We have something we call a 'drip file`. If you have a no, put them in the drip file, which is a place where you can continually work with them over a long time frame.... Keep following up. We were in that drip file for three years and had bits of information continually dripped to us. Stay connected with them with a simple, "How`s it going?"

Stay visible on social media with very regular posting, commenting, and liking. Have a system organized so you know to search them out periodically on social media to be visible to them on their profiles. Every drip contact goes back in the drip file at the beginning of the year so that you can continue to drip/ follow up with them. This way, they never get lost in the busyness of the business or swamped in social media. If it is still a no, no problem, we just keep at it. We followed up with a woman for ten years, and finally her circumstances had changed over that time, and she was finally a yes. Her husband is gone, she is with a new man and he wants to build a business. Staying connected for so long, she is now open and ready. It`s the long game. Don`t judge and don`t presuppose. It is not a "no, never". It just is a "not right now" and they go back into the drip file.

Be kind-hearted enough in your business to understand that you don`t need to know the reason behind the first or second no. We don`t know what is going on behind closed doors. That is what keeps us going back to following up. Maybe their circumstances have changed. Maybe their thinking has changed. Ours certainly did.

Our Purpose Helps Others Build Theirs

We have a mission statement and based on that alone, people join us. You are on this planet for something bigger, something bigger than yourself. How big is your why? What are you willing to commit to, to make a bigger impact?

"Making a difference by impacting lives today for future healthier generations" is our mission. Our first mission statement was ``It`s all about making a difference," which was our guiding force. But more recently, thought Leader Simon Sinek (The Infinite Game 2019) explains the need to share with people the vision of the Infinite Game...legacy. Knowing that well after they have contributed, their work will live on.

We are in an interesting time right now as so many new methodologies are emerging to build networks. The opportunities are endless, global, and easy to build using smartphones and social media platforms. It`s easier to meet people than ever before online. The principles of old are still important though, and they include personal relationships and friendships. The opportunity to share a meal, co-host a Zoom or hold a Facebook event live makes it very simple and fun. We hope we never lose these timeless personal relationships within this industry.

One of the most powerful follow ups you can do is with your leaders. Staying connected on a very regular basis is key. They also need to know you value their input into your business and likewise value your input into theirs. Our favorite method is spending quality time at events! Travel has always been a huge motivator for us to build a global business, and to travel with our leaders is fun, exciting and rewarding. So much heart connection is built.

Encouraging your prospects and team members/leaders to dream bigger is essential. In a busy and sometimes chaotic world. Helping others to see possibility and planting a vision becomes important. We need to consistently look for the positive and ask questions... What drives you? What would you do with an additional $1000, $5000, $10,000 per month? What would your life look like? How much a difference would this income make for you? It is so important for all new leaders to focus on the dreams and as much personal development as possible. Seek out mentors, leaders and writers that inspire you to be, do, and have more.

Leadership is a choice and a responsibility. It`s also a joy and incredibly rewarding experience in this industry. Stepping up into higher levels of leadership is important. Seek out incredible industry coaches like Rob Sperry. Be prepared to be challenged; to grow; to fail forward

You are in the right spot right now to start a business. You have the right tools right now to start a business. This book is one of those tools. If we could leave you with one thing, it would be to remember this - Be brave enough to have the conversation and bold enough to follow up. Set your sails and go with the wind.

Coaches Notes: John Maxwell says the greatest ability one can have is the ability to learn how to learn. These two incredible leaders have that uncanny ability to learn how to learn. They understood that this business is all about short-term urgency balanced with long-term vision. This is a tough balance. If you have too much short-term urgency, sometimes you panic when you have a bad month or quarter. If you have too much long-term vision without the short-term vision, you never have any sense of urgency to get things done. My challenge for you is to commit to five years to this incredible profession just like Charlie and Annie did. Don`t just read this book, but implement the incredible lessons taught!

Author: Gary Stern

- Built an organization of 18k+ distributors and customers in fifteen countries worldwide.

- Team responsible for close to ten million dollars in revenue & four and a half million in commissions over the past decade.

- Made it to the Elite Ranks of company in three years.

- First and only company for ten years now.

- Established speaker/trainer at company conventions on multiple occasions.

- 2x internationally published author

- Podcaster and trainer for *The Game of Networking* and **MLM** Nation.

- Five-time State of Florida cycling champion.

"Dream Big, Make it Happen!!"

The Future's So Bright
In Network Marketing!!!

I just got off the phone with a new distributor who is thrilled that there is an option like network marketing out there for her. She is a school principal and with the times we`re now living in, she doesn`t want to go back to work. She doesn`t want to bring home any sickness from school to her newborn, her three year old, or to her husband who has cardiovascular complications. She sees the opportunity with network marketing, and she doesn`t want to go into a school that could be life threatening for her family. It gets me so excited that she has this option. There is a solution for her to make money without having to face that real fear daily. It`s truly amazing that I get to show her a different way of earning money that does not compromise her or her family`s health.

This fires me up because health and wellness have always been important to me. They`ve been a big driver in my life. My professional background includes working as a physical therapist and as a pharmaceutical rep. I loved physical therapy and being able to help others. uld do about it. I was working with professional athletes from all over the world. I hated what the insurance companies did to the profession. I felt hopeless, like there was nothing I could do about it.

Then, my mom and dad both got sick with cancer at the same time. They were divorced and living in completely different cities. When my dad passed away, it was a wakeup call to my life. I quit my job overnight and moved back to Florida to take care of my mom. It completely freaked me out to think I could lose her. It was then that I learned about leverage. I loved my job, but I had to quit it in order to take care of my mom. I went into pharmaceuticals so I could have some free time on the side. As much as being a rep was rewarding financially, it wasn`t what I wanted. I was still working for someone else. I constantly had Big Brother looking over my shoulder. It simply wasn`t me, and it wasn`t congruent with the life that I wanted to create.

It was then that I was introduced to network marketing. My cycling coach, Simon, shared it with me and it just clicked. I was still skeptical of the business side of it and started off rather slowly. But the idea was exactly what I was looking for. In just a few years, I hit the upper ranks in my company. I was at a place of seeing what leverage truly looked and felt like. I LOVED IT!

I can`t imagine doing anything but network marketing. I had said no twenty eight times before finally saying yes to network marketing. TWENTY-EIGHT times! And one of those no`s was my best friend! I don`t kick myself for saying no that many times, but I wish I had been a bit more open-minded. I landed in network marketing at the perfect time with the perfect people and the perfect message. I feel like I am still at the right place at the right time. You are, too, because you are reading this book! Be open minded to this being the perfect time to read this book, read this chapter, and implement some of the things I am going to share with you.

Coaches notes- Gary has that contagious energy that everyone wants to be around. He is one of those types of people you would put on your chicken list to contact. Gary saying no twenty eight times should give you perspective.

1. They typically aren`t saying no to you, so don`t take it personally.
2. We never know when it will be the right time, so never give up on anyone.
3. Stay in contact with those who reject you. Respect their decision to not buy your products or join your team, but ask them if you can stay in contact and keep them apprised of what`s going on. You just never know when the timing will change and they will be ready.

You Can't Buy This

Trust and belief can't be bought. They must be earned. At the time I was introduced to network marketing, I had won four state time trial championships in cycling and had another one coming up in a matter of months. Simon, my cycling coach, said, "There is something I want to share with you that will help you with recovery." I was hesitant, but not really. He was my coach. I had hired him to teach and train me. And I trusted him.

Trust is so important early on. You've got to earn people's trust. "People don't care how much you know, until they know how much you care." I knew Simon cared about me. Even though I sniffed out that it was one of those 'network marketing things,' I trusted him to have my best interest at heart. Though I had said no to network marketing twenty eight times before this, I was open to what he had to say because I trusted him.

It was the science that blew me away. It was in my wheelhouse and came from someone I trusted, so I said yes. I had no idea what I was doing. I still didn't really believe in the business, but I decided to give it a go. At a minimum, I was going to tell everyone I knew and loved about this incredible product because I truly believed that it would help them. You have to have that belief. Trust and belief can't be bought. They must be earned.

So how do you earn trust and belief with friends, colleagues, and even people you don't know? It is all about attraction marketing. One of the first things you need to do is to be the authentic and honest YOU. Rob Sperry taught me this. When I was going from predominantly offline recruiting to recruiting online, I reached out to a group of people to help me. People with experience and results. Rob was one of them. When he talked to me about getting online, it just made sense. It was some of the best advice I ever received in my ten-year network marketing career.

Be the authentic and honest you. Don't portray yourself as someone you are not. I am the same person offline and online. My life is the same wherever you see me. Earn trust by being authentic.

People do business with people they like and trust. At a given company, we all have the same products/services. We all have the same opportunity. It is the same for everyone. The differentiator is YOU. If you are one type of person on social media and a completely different person offline, people will figure it out. If you say one thing but do another, people will figure it out. They won't trust you. Heck, they may even start to talk to others about how you can't be trusted.

Be you and be authentic to yourself. Don't live in the past by posting pictures of you from five years ago. Be relatable by being who you are now. I can't relate to someone who flies on a private jet all the time. It's cool, but I can't relate. Be relatable. Tell your relatable story. If you are struggling, share that struggle. Don't whine about it. Share the struggle and the steps you're taking to overcome it or how you overcame it. You have to be Rocky. If you don't have a particular story that relates, then use someone else's. They want you in their corner, because they trust you. Nobody wants to partner with a person who isn't trustworthy or relatable.

Coaches Notes: These are timeless principles that Gary is teaching. If you can't trust yourself, how can others trust you? I learned a valuable lesson years ago from one of the most successful people I know. He asked this question, "What is the most important thing you can do to build confidence?" I gave many different answers, but his response has stuck with me. "Do what you say you are going to do when you say you are going to do it. This will build trust within yourself and build trust with others. It will change your world." The hardest person you are ever going to recruit into network marketing is yourself, but that person is also the only person you will ever need to recruit. Once you truly recruit yourself, everything else will fall into place.

Attract To Sell

Attraction marketing is super simple. Be more INTERESTED than interesting. Now, let me be clear. That doesn't mean you can drop the part of being interesting. It matters, and I want to touch on that first. Find out who you are and what your brand is. You have to be interesting up front, but it doesn't stop there. You have to be interested in others, as well. So, who are you? I am dynamic, energetic, outgoing. I am a financial guru. I almost became a financial advisor. I was in the medical field for years. I'm passionate about healthy living, exercise, and true wellness. Like Rob talks about in *The Game of Networking*, be recallable. Be the guy or gal that people can remember.

So, here is an exercise for you. Think about being recallable. What are the top five things people are going to remember about you? People know I am a family guy. That is my #1 thing I want people to know. My top five are family guy, financial and health guru, adventurer, traveler, and cyclist/surfer. That is my wheelhouse. Brand who you are. Take your top five things and start posting about them.

It is ok to not attract everyone. If there is someone out there who is unmotivated and wants to just sit around all day, I am probably not their guy. That's OK. I want to attract the go-getters. People who are looking for a change. People who are like me and want to live like me. Know who you are. Stick to your authentic self and brand. Be that person over and over again.

In order to attract people, you need to have a clearly-defined person or 'avatar'. Get out there and actively look for that person you need and want to be associated with. I am out there looking for family guys who want to do more with their lives. This guy wants more experiences, but he doesn`t know how. He`s out there looking for solutions but hasn`t found them yet. I want to be interested in his life. Is he wanting to increase his lifestyle? Does he want to spend more time with his family? Does he want to travel more? Does he want to spend less time in the office? Or bag the office life all together to have more control and freedom over his life? I must be interested in him and knowing what he is all about. I am interested in finding out his wants, pains, hopes, dreams, and desires.

This Isn't Monkey Business

Engage with people who you want to work with and be interested in them. When I say interested in them, I mean engage with them. My business was initially built to the higher ranks offline, which gave me experience connecting with people face to face. But, it wasn`t until I started using and engaging online that my business took off. Let me be clear when we talk about engaging online. A monkey can scroll and click 'like`. Don`t kid yourself; that is not engaging. ENGAGE!

Have your list of your top 25 people that you would like to attract into your business. Implement a system to actively engage with them. Go on Facebook and star these folks so that you see their feed first. If my objective is to engage with people, then I better do everything I can to engage. That includes seeing their posts when they post. This list is your priority people who you want to attract to your business. They are the top people you want to engage with. I`m not just going to like their posts, I am going to engage. These are people who I saw as like-minded, who I was attracted to, and who I want in my business. Of course I am going to go in and engage.

There was this woman who was adventurous. She went through grief like me. She showed leadership qualities by managing a tight team in the defense industry. She seemed like someone I wanted to engage with. She just bought a sailboat and is cruising up the east coast of the United States. My goal when I engage with her online is to stay front-of-mind with her. To stay recallable. To attract her into my business. When she recently made the decision to join my team as a brand-new business partner, she highlighted my engaging follow up as a key reason why.

Take a platform and master it. I love Facebook. I used it first and mastered it before moving on to Instagram and LinkedIn. Maybe YouTube, Snapchat or TikTok is your thing. Whichever one you choose, master it before moving on. If it`s Facebook, stop right now and set your top 25 people to follow first. Engage in their posts everyday or every other day. The more you engage, the more they will see you. If you are putting out posts that they like, then they will want to connect with you. I love to share experiences with my followers that they find attracting. I sell my life`s experiences to them. The people I attract are the ones who connect with my passions and life experiences.

The Very Basics

There are some basics with attraction marketing. Go study it. Go learn it. Learn from someone that has already been there. It will cut your failing time down. As Rob always says, we all 'suck` at the beginning. You`ve got to crawl before you can walk. And walk before you can run. And run before you can sprint to win the race.

Do the basics. I have seen people who are at higher ranks in my own company who have pictures of multiple people or an animal as their profile photo on social media. Don`t do this! People can`t relate to you if they can`t see you. First impressions are everything. Get a clear picture of yourself for your profile picture on all social media platforms. It sounds simple, but it is crazy how many people overlook this step.

Your cover photo shouldn`t be a company billboard. Think about what is going to attract people to you and help them get to know you. Look at your profile and ask, "Is this the kind of person I want to do business with and hang out with? Can I trust this person?" If you don`t answer yes, then you need to do a cleanse on social media. Find a good picture to use as your profile and a cover photo that helps people get to know you. One that invites them in. Then, send your profile to your besties and ask them for their honest feedback. Not what you want to hear, but what you need to hear. This is your calling card. You want the open feedback to optimize your outreach. I`ve learned that this has helped me improve and leverage my skills.

4-Step Dmo Attraction Marketing Plan

Using attraction marketing is so simple. It is something I teach my team as part of our DMO or daily method of operation. It puts your business on autopilot. It systematizes it. Best of all, it simplifies it. Before I share more on this, there is something that is crucial to your success. You can't just do these steps. You must TRACK them! "What gets measured gets done." Remember that! What gets measured gets done. Here is a simple four-step DMO attraction marketing plan:

1) Create a schedule of Facebook posts you will make personally. Make yourself seen using those five top things that are authentic to you. The ones that people are attracted to.

2) Add new people. You need to be adding three to five new people a day. Again, it can be done in person. That counts. I always ask people if they are on Facebook and would like to connect there. Don't take a day off. Be consistent. If you do this 300 days a year, you have added 900+ new people over the course of the year. That is huge!! That right there will help you break through.

3) Comment every day on a minimum of five posts. It doesn't mean liking a post. It means engaging. Go back to the top 25 list. These are the people who you want to engage with. Make sure you use Messenger also to wish people a happy birthday. Do this daily! The key is when you wish them happy birthday, ask them a question at the same time. For example, "Happy Birthday John! What are you most looking forward to this next year?" or "What are your big plans for the next 12 months?" It is much more ENGAGING than the standard birthday wish!

4) Minimum of one ask a day. Three is average. Five or more asks per day is rockstar status. This is just an invite to look. "Are you open to take a look?" You will be attracting new people. When you start putting out the invites, you will come to a place when the yeses start pouring in. Done daily, this is over 300 to 1500 new leads per year! This is the time to add them into your sales funnel or system. Let the system do the heavy lifting for you since it`s duplicable. "Systems don`t fail people, people fail systems."

Last summer I got very focused about doing my DMO. I went into "conquering mode" like Rob talks about in *The Game of Conquering*. I wanted to conquer the business. I did my DMO every day. I brought on seven new distributors and eight new customers in a single month. That is the first time I have ever brought in that many people in a single month. Crazy! It was the DMO. A consistent run of my DMO made all the difference. Doing the DMO consistently pays off exponentially. We all want to have balanced business. That is where having a simple DMO and doing it consistently comes into play. It will propel you to the next rank in your company.

Lasting Light And Impact

We live in a negative world right now. Network marketing is a source of positivity and light. Your work is directly correlated to your own personal growth. Are you working on being a better human? I had two "Self Help" books when I started this profession. Now, I have a library with hundreds of personal development books since committing to personal growth seven years ago. When people told me it`s all about becoming the person you want to attract, I thought they were crazy. Now I am addicted to personal growth. That is also part of my DMO. Feeding my brain with "good stuff" every day. In fact, it`s how I start every day.

If you see that you have a learning gap and don`t know how to do some of these things, no sweat! Don`t let that hold you back. We all have gaps. It is not where the gap is, but how you decide to close it that matters. There is no better way to close the gap than seeking out guidance and mentorship. I sought out leaders in my own company. I wasn`t just paying attention to WHAT they were doing, but HOW they were doing it. I reached out to coaches and mentors like Rob. I had to learn how leaders like them carried themselves. Your upline will never get upset with you asking questions. If they do, find a new upline. Find the upline that is willing to see your initiative of asking questions as an asset. Be proactive and learn how to learn. Earn the title of leader. Close the gap so you can show others how to do it. It is pure duplication.

I want as many people to experience this as possible. Imagine what the world would look like if more people did what we did. If more people thought like we did. It would move the needle more towards positivity and light. When you learn and start doing it, you instinctively want to teach others how to do the same. But first, YOU have to go out and do it. Then train others how to do it. Finally, train others to train others how to do it. It`s your big dreamer & doer Gary Stern signing out. Remember to "Dream Big, Make it Happen!"

Coaches Notes: Gary is one of those people I connected with right away. I watched him do this same kind of genuine connection over and over again at the seven-figure mastermind this summer. He is someone you just want to be friends with. He doesn`t just teach attraction marketing, but he lives inside and outside his business. His strategies work. Go assess where you are strong and weak on attraction marketing. Then create a game plan on which one strategy that Gary laid out you are going to implement. If you continue to do this eventually you will become great at attraction marketing and begin to grow your business to a whole new level.

Author: Julie Stoll-Kelly

- International team of over 35k and rising!

- Eleven years ago she lived in a home with no furniture and slept on an air mattress.

- Does a gratitude call every bonus payday and has witnessed many tears of happiness because of the lives that have been positively impacted.

- Earned trips to Cancun, South Africa, & a Southern Caribbean Cruise.

- Former Realtor

I am in competition with no one

I run my own race.

I have no desire to play the game of being better than anyone in any way, shape or form

I just aim to improve to be better than I was before

I am me & I am free

-Jenny Perry

When I started with my current company, I told my sponsor, half-joking, "Can you call the CEO and let her know I am going to blow this up?!!" My amazing, sweet, soft spoken sponsor didn`t know how to respond to that. She also didn`t know that I was being serious about my level of commitment to the business.

I had that type of confidence, because I knew I had the secret of success! I had the right system, the right culture, the right posture, the right product, and the right mindset! I knew that if I showed people that they could do this business AND be unapologetically themselves, there would be a huge market of people willing to give it a try.

There have been so many stigmas about network marketing. People think that other people that do network marketing are naggy and only focused on sales and more sales. They think that it is a scam or a "get rich quick" scheme. We know it is none of those things, and that the people that do network marketing are just people! Regular people trying their hand at success!

So why do we concern ourselves so much with what people think? Part of it is because at one point or another, we may have been thinking the same thing. We don`t want to show up and have people think we are only trying to make a sale. We worry about what they will put in the comments. We worry about how we will look, and what if I stutter over my words? We are so worried about what other people are going to think, and It holds us back. It causes us to freeze and not get started! After working with so many people I realized that if I could get everyone to figure out the answer to one question, it could help them solve the majority of their worry. So, the real question is, "How can I market my product/opportunity and still remain true to who I am?"

If you knew you could be yourself, and make money doing it, how many people would raise their hand and say yes? A LOT! You can do it. You can be yourself and build a business. The first thing that you need to start doing is be unapologetically YOU! Be yourself, and people will thank you for it. Be yourself and people will want to do business with you. Be yourself unapologetically and your business will thrive. People love to watch someone have success and their story is relatable. When we are ourselves and show people our story, it makes it seem attainable for them in their own lives.

I have ADHD, and I am very hyper. I don`t drink coffee or caffeine because who knows what would come of that! Being hyper and happy is just who I am! My whole life I have heard I am too much. I say too much, I say it too fast, I say it too loud. I go one step too far. Before network marketing, I had always thought that I needed to hold myself back from being me. It never felt good to think that being me was a bad thing that needed to be corrected all the time. I was ashamed of who I was and tried to be someone...less.

When I started with network marketing, it was like I was given permission to just be me. It was freeing. I get to be me all the time with everyone. I can get on a Facebook live, and forget my pants! People say, "Oh Julie is crazy." And to me, it doesn`t sound like a bad word. (Totally happened, by the way!)

People like to do business with like-minded people. People like to see the real you and be a part of your life because you have something they want in their own life. People like the behind-the-scenes of our lives, because they want to connect with us and who we really are. Being unapologetically you seems like the exact opposite of what some people on social media are telling you to do. But I promise, being you is the best practice you can put into place when you are on social media. You attract your tribe! If you are positive and happy, you attract positive and happy! If you are negative, you attract negativity.

I am going to share with you, some of the systems I use with my own team to help them start to post and be yourself online and in person.

Coaches Notes: Julie is one of those people we all love to be around. She has found a way to step into her greatness which I know all of us have. If you follow her closely, you will see her posting very funny videos of herself and her team. She not only attracts those who resonate with her style. but she also creates culture by doubling down her uniqueness. Give yourself permission to be the BOLD version of YOU. God didn't send you to this earth to be average!

5,4,3,2,1....Do It!

I have a system within my team where they can share when they are going live, so everyone on the team can help support them. The newest member can post something like, "Doing my first Facebook live today at 3:00 pm CT, and I am so nervous so please jump on and support me!" That new team member knows they have the support from everyone telling them good luck and commenting on that post, but it also gives everyone on the team an opportunity to jump on at 3:00 pm if they want and encourage her while she is on live. This helps our team stay connected and helps our newest members launch. Everyone feels supported and empowered. It can also help that new person get more engagements on the live, and we all know, more views and comments means Facebook will let even more people see it.

One of the biggest fears that the newest person tells me about getting on and doing a live is, "I don`t know what I am going to say!"

"Great!," I tell them, "Get on and tell your audience! Tell them you are nervous! Everyone can relate to that! Even I was afraid in the beginning to just push the start of a live."

I remember the first time I hit the button to go live. It made me scared because maybe my family or my husband or even his friend were going to watch me! But you need to remember, that is the point. You want people to be watching you. It doesn`t need to be perfect or scripted. It just needs to be you. Start small and work your way up to longer recordings. You just need to jump in and do it. Use the 5,4,3,2,1 method.

Here is how to do it. Sit in front of your screen with your Facebook app open with the live ready to go. Take a deep breath and count backward from five. 5,4,3,2,1 and then push the button to go live. It really is that simple. Start off simple. Say hi to everyone and tell them about the weather. Tell them you are nervous or tell them what your kids are up to today. Keep it simple. You can do Facebook live, Instagram live, a Tik Tok. Whatever platform you are most drawn to, start there.

The idea is to get used to pushing the button and talking. Keep it short and authentic to you. I don`t like scripts. People can see right through that. Just be you. Be yourself and keep being yourself. Get used to pushing the button and talking.

A lot of times when I go live, it isn`t about my business. I`ll buy something funny on Amazon and share it. I`ll subscribe to a box and unbox it in front of my audience. I just get on and talk to people about what is going on with me or with them if they want to engage. I don`t tell my team what to say or how to say it, because then it wouldn`t be about them. I want them to be themselves. It misses the point if I tell people "Be you, but here is your script."

Launch yourself into your business by using this method! It`s ok if you are scared and worried about putting yourself out there. You can still post or go live and be scared. You just have to do it, and spoiler alert, you will live through it! Stick to the system above and stay focused on two things; pushing the button and talking.

Being unapologetically myself has been my gift to myself and others. People will see a post and tell me how much they love my energy, and they have trouble scrolling past without adding their comment! Due to the pandemic, people are scared right now, because there is a lot of uncertainty, fear, job loss, cutbacks. When they jump on my lives, they can escape for the next 10 minutes and just laugh. I answer questions and I talk about whatever comes to mind. I am of course selling my product, but I am also selling the lifestyle, a friendship – something that is priceless. I love telling people about being in a company that loves me for being me. I talk about the feeling of being included and not being scared. So many women and men are looking for friends, looking for something that is "theirs," looking for inclusion with a great comp plan attached!

> **Coaches Notes:** Yes, Facebook Lives can be incredibly scary! So let`s challenge that fear. Is your why a lie? Is your why bigger than your fears? If someone told you that if you did two Facebook Lives every week for two years and after that your business would generate enough income to fulfill your dreams, would you do it? Now,of course, I am not making claims. I am only challenging you to follow Julie`s advice and face your fears!!! One of the key reasons I started The Game of Networking Facebook group is so that people in network marketing could connect and share their struggles and wins in a group of people that get it. You aren`t alone if you have a fear, but what are you going to do about it? Check out The Game of Networking Facebook group to see how others face and conquer their fears.

People Want To Hang Out With You

Put thought behind your post. Anytime you go to engage with your audience by making a post, stop for a moment and think, "If I post this, will it stop someone in my audience from just scrolling by? Will it make them want to see more of me?" If you can answer yes, post it! If not, work on the content for a bit, OR scrap it.

The main objective is always going to be to sell. People want to buy products, but they want the feeling they will get more than the product. That is why they are buying from you. You are selling people on having an experience with you. What do you want that experience to be? Really think about that. Because that usually is one of the first things to go out the window when someone signs up for network marketing. They become an infomercial that no one wants to engage with. Be real. Keep it engaging.

Try this today- go and pick a favorite vacation spot that you have. Post a picture of that spot and ask people what their favorite vacation spot is. It is incredible the engagement you can get from being real and posting something like this. Put on some lashes, lippy, and do your hair and tell everyone how beautiful you feel! Your audience will look at that picture and notice your confidence. They want confidence! They will notice your happiness. They want happiness! They will tell you how beautiful you look, they want that too! It isn`t always about selling the product. It is about engaging with people and getting them to know you as you get to know them. Make them want what you have! Make them want to be your best friend!

I have done one hundred and twelve Zoom calls this month with my team and they have all been about the same thing. I want to share with you what those calls have all been about. You must clean up your Facebook profile picture! Don`t have a picture of a cat or a group picture where someone can`t identify who you are. People want to connect with you, but they have to see who they are connecting to. Your profile picture is people`s first introduction to you. You only get one chance at a first impression, so make it good!

You also have to stop sharing other people`s creative posts and create your own! You may come across a great post or something that you think your audience would love, but don`t be lazy and just share it to your page. That actually takes your audience away from you. Take the time to put your own spin on it and create your own content that will have others sharing it and driving traffic to you. Every interaction, including your profile, is saying something about you. You want people to think, "hey, I want to hang out with her! I want her to be MY best friend!"

You have to keep your page clean and take a good hard look at what people are seeing when they click on your profile for the first time. If you came onto your own page, would you want to be best friends with the person you see? If you have a page that is unapologetically yourself, people can start to relate to you and your vibe attracts your tribe!

The "Give and Get" method is also very important. If your audience posts, you need to engage on their post if you expect them to come engage on your posts! It`s only fair! Then, when they engage on your post, you need to reply back and create the relationship. For instance, take a look at the last time you posted. When people left a comment, did you engage with them? Or, did you leave them hanging out thinking you don`t care? Always comment on every single comment that people leave on your own post. It keeps people engaged and they want to comment more when they know that you are commenting on your post.

Just because you have a great product or opportunity doesn't mean you need to post about it every day and talk about it every post. In fact, make sure your posts aren't all about your product and business! You can keep people more engaged by keeping it real and about you. We also love to post motivation. It is awesome to see what people engage with. For my team, we have created content that they can share for the first thirty-one days of business. Create your own thirty one day challenge and see if you can come up with fun engaging content for a month.

Your Audience Isn't You

Your audience isn't always going to like or comment on everything you do or say, and that's ok. We are meant to be different. Don't see that as a bad thing. Be unapologetically you!

I have always been a confident person. I would read books that said things like, "You are worth it!" and I would think to myself, "Yeah, I know that." It has been an obstacle for me to see that so many women struggle with not feeling confident. But I realized that it was ok for me to be confident, and it was ok for others to not be confident at all. I always focus on how I can help them with that confidence. It is perfect that we aren't the same because I can teach them about confidence and there is plenty that they can teach me about!

I had to learn how to be an active listener and be empathetic with where other people are at, even if it isn't something that I struggle with. I have a zero-tolerance for negativity. That doesn't mean that my team doesn't raise concern when needed. It simply means that I want solutions! My zero tolerance for negativity means that we look at issues from all angels and look at how we can find a solution and move forward. Being able to work this way has helped me see people for who they are and always find the best in them and find solutions that are best for everyone when we have things come up. Use this zero-tolerance policy as you look at your social media. What good does it do to be posting negativity on your feed or in the comments of someone else's post? Usually it doesn't. If you see a problem, be open and find the solution.

Whether your team or your audience, it's the same. You may not connect with everything, but you can actively listen to them and their experiences and find a connection authentically through that.

I am such a goer, and everyone's personality is different. I want the top! Sometimes, I have to slow down and actively listen to people to see what their "top" is. My mentors have taught me to slow down and love everyone where they are at. The leaders within my team teach me about different techniques for success. They teach me how to be a better me, daily! I am a student to each of them and I have learned so much. They may have signed with me, but I am grateful for their lesson I have learned from them as well! I am never done learning!

I have a lot of people come to me and say that they don't know how to work with different personalities. It all comes back to being an active listener. Don't try to answer or fix a problem until you know the root of the conversation. The root of the concern may not even be what that person initially brought to your attention. Listen to why they are doing things a certain way. Listen to how they are seeing things. Most of the time, it makes all the difference for people to just be heard.

The best part about working with different personalities is that we can all strengthen each other when we work together. I have team members that have incredible strengths that I don't have, and I love them for it. They fill in the gaps that I have, and I fill in theirs. That is why this business works so well. We can see the differences, but not make that mean we are different or not able to work together.

A huge key to my success is not always being a great recruiter myself, but finding the matched energy by driving the line. I work with all levels if they want to work! Drive the line, be an active listener, accept people where they are in the business, and match their energy!

Remember how I told you about my sponsor calling the CEO? Well, I reached the very top of the company in ten weeks. My team accomplished this by using our step-by step-system on Facebook. That was it! The exact methods I shared with you in this chapter got me to the top of the company.

It wasn`t some complex formula that got me there. It wasn`t working 24/7 that got me there. It was not easy but SIMPLE. We worked with confidence, excitement, and an unshaken belief in knowing that we could impact a lot of lives with our opportunity. I showed up authentically as myself, got to know others, and shared my heart with my audience!

I have been with companies that have told me I was too much. I have been left out of things in this industry for not conforming to the standard set by people within the company. It just wasn`t a fit, and when I realized that I could build a network marketing business AND be myself, I found true success. You can have a system and still remain true to being unapologetically you!

Coaches Notes: The sooner you realize that all of these strategies work, when you get over yourself and your ego, the sooner your business will thrive! Julie is as bold as it gets. Each one of you has that uniqueness that needs to show. Part of becoming the best version of you is to create non-negotiables. Julie created a key non-negotiable for herself and her team. She does not accept any negativity. Being negative brings yourself and everyone else around you down. You must create your non-negotiables to protect your dreams, goals and aspirations. Once you do, then negotiate with yourself to demand success from the world!

CONCLUSION

As you finish this incredible book, I have one last piece of advice for you. Do NOT become the broke know-it-all.

One of the biggest issues network marketers face is focusing too much on the learning aspect and not taking enough action. You can`t watch 100 videos on YouTube on how to become great at playing the piano and expect to be great. You have to actually practice playing the piano. The same goes for network marketing.

The strategies that you just discovered from this book work. They will help you tremendously in your business, but only if you focus on applying them consistently.

When I started in this business, my mentor taught me one thing that made a massive difference to how I was showing up. He asked me, "Is what you are doing right now making you the most amount of money?" Go and write this down and put it in your office or wherever you are working on your business. "Is what I am doing right now making me the most amount of money?"

This statement will help keep you focused on applying the strategies you just learned.

Thank you for investing the time into reading or listening to me and these incredible authors.

Thank you for investing in yourself.

If you haven`t already grabbed all the bonuses mentioned in this book, do so before you forget.

www.sperrybonus.com

Lastly, I want to give gratitude to the authors of this book. These are amazing leaders, and they are incredible human beings. I am honored to help mentor them and even more honored to call them friends. Thank you for your contribution. Thank you for inspiring me and so many others to be better!

Rob Sperry